Plants

WITH

Superpowers

75 Remarkable Plants for
your Garden and Home

DAVID DOMONEY

FRANCES
LINCOLN

Contents

Plants bestow many things upon us, but the first must be wonder.

Do you remember the school science project of planting a bean inside a jam jar and watching in amazement through the glass as it transformed into a plant, springing into life with a single root and a shoot? I still feel that same sense of excitement and wonder whenever a seedling is germinating in my greenhouse. The natural world continually bestows on us the purest source of happiness.

Childhood is enriched with learning new and incredible things, but as we grow older and wiser, our fascination with nature tends to hold nostalgic memories as well. The scent of spruce reminds us of Christmas trees, freshly mown lawn triggers the memory of the school playing fields being cut. The sight of autumn leaves, burnished bright against the gloom, signals the end of another summer, and pulling an apple from a tree elicits a smile echoing a distant childhood memory of tree climbing and eating something that does not come wrapped in plastic. Some plants become special to us, symbolic and personally sacred, as they are custodians of the emotional triggers they command.

No matter your age, however, this book delivers seventy-five wonderous plants that I hope will instil that same childhood sense of amazement and inspiration into nature's marvels you enjoyed in abundance as you were first learning about this wonderful world: plants that grow incredibly fast; some that shoot seeds like bullets; others that can change colour or move independently; some that not only have a memory but can use it to count too; while another can survive an atomic bomb.

These plants that are alive and living on our planet today produce a tapestry of tales – some dating back hundreds of millions of years, others more recent. Many are intricately woven into the evolution of humanity as our ancestors developed physically and socially. The abilities and uses of many of these plants are at the very core of nearly all the great human civilizations in history, and their symbolic representations remain just as revered and sacred today.

Neither are they all rare plants from faraway jungles or distant mountain ranges on the edge of the world. No, these seventy-five plants can almost all be found in garden centres and plant retail stores.

As you delve into this book of incredible plants, you'll experience disbelief, awe, amazement, and, I hope, a belief that nature has many secrets for you to discover and enjoy, awakening the fascination of your child within.

David Domoney

Introduction

Superpower: **Sub-Aqua Survival**

Marimo moss balls

Aegagropila linnaei
Native to Japan and northern Europe

Marimo moss balls are found in the lakes of Japan, Iceland, Scotland, Estonia and Australia, where they have been known to live for more than two centuries. Most days, they leave the lakebed to rise through the water to the surface, where they bob about a bit before sinking back to the bottom. The word 'Marimo' comes from Japanese – *mari* being a bouncy play ball and *mo* a generic term for plants that grow in water. Although these plants are known colloquially as moss balls, they are in fact made up of pure algae. However, they do not attach themselves to rocks or substrate, but are instead moved about by the lake's undercurrents. Such rolling back and forth in the water helps form their spherical shape, yet there is no central stone or pip inside. They float and sink according to light conditions, rising to conduct photosynthesis.

Appearance
These peculiar little plants look like moss-covered stones; in the water, they have an attractive, almost furry appearance, thanks to the algae reaching out like small hairs. They are typically a lovely bright shade of mossy-green and grow to the size of a tennis ball, though larger specimens have been found. However, when available commercially, you won't see them much larger than 5cm (2in) in diameter.

Uses
Marimo moss balls can be kept as 'pets' – there is something almost sentient about their habits – in fresh or lightly salted water, in glass vases, bottles or aquariums. In Japan, they are protected and believed to bring great fortune. They are also becoming increasingly popular, with many specialist garden centres and florists now selling them.

Interesting Facts
- In Japan, the indigenous Ainu people hold a three-day festival in Hokkaido every year in October to honour marimo moss balls.
- Japan has protected this species since the 1920s.
- Marimo moss balls require little care and have been described as family heirlooms because they live so long.

Growing Tips
Marimo moss balls will grow better in cool temperatures. Keep them fully submerged in water, which should be changed every two weeks for most of the year, and more frequently in summer. Tap water can be used. Keep the tank in low to medium indirect light away from radiators to avoid the marimo turning brown. Should they turn white this indicates that they are exposed to too much light. Carbonated soda water can be added to help increase photosynthesis. To help retain the rounded shape, periodically gently agitate the water. Marimo benefits from being given a gentle wash every few weeks when changing the water. Gently squeeze the water out of the marimo, then rinse; do this a few times until the squeezed water runs clear.

Superpower: **Cleansing**

Horse chestnut

Aesculus hippocastanum
Native to Albania, Bulgaria, Greece,
Turkey, Turkmenistan and Yugoslavia

Collected and coveted by generations of children, there is something magical about the fruit of the horse chestnut tree. Hidden inside spiny-cased pods, waiting to be liberated by nimble fingers, lie beautiful, mahogany-brown conkers. The contrast between the prickly, dull-green armour and the shiny treasure within makes the conker even more special. Yet there is more magic within: the conker fruit provides a type of natural soap. It's believed the Vikings used them to stay clean-ish. The active ingredient is saponin, which works as a handy organic detergent for lifting dirt and grease. You'll sometimes find it added to shampoos and shower gels. On autumn days when horse chestnuts drop their conkers onto wet roads and they get mashed up by passing cars, you'll sometimes see soap bubbles forming amid the debris as if someone has spilled detergent. In fact, it's the naturally foaming saponins from inside the conkers.

Appearance

Horse chestnut trees reach an ultimate height of 40m (130ft) and live for up to 300 years. The fruit of this tree, conkers transform radically depending what growing stage they are in. They start as white and pink blossoms produced by the trees, which are pollinated by insects. These develop into green, spiky husks, inside which the seed grows. Eventually, these husks fall from the trees or are knocked down by cheeky squirrels, birds or children. If they aren't cracked open by the fall, you can split the husk to find the glossy conkers tucked away inside. These shiny seeds vary in size, but all tend to be roughly spherical shape with a flattish top and a whitish crown.

Uses

Making your own conker soap to use as a washing detergent is simple. First, wrap your conkers in a tea towel and crush them with a hammer or rolling pin. You can break them down further by using a coffee grinder or blender if you have one handy. Move your crushed conkers into a heat-resistant container, such as a Pyrex measuring jug, and pour in hot water, to a ratio of one part horse chestnuts and two parts hot water. Leave for at least 30 minutes then strain through a fine mesh sieve or cheesecloth, to separate the liquid from the solid conker remains. Dispose of the solids. The remaining solution is your liquid conker soap. Store in a sealed container in the refrigerator for up to a week.

Interesting Facts

- The horse chestnut tree is so named because of the curved stalks of the leaves. In autumn, when the foliage falls, arched scars are left behind, which look like little horseshoes.
- You can identify conker trees in winter because they have shiny, sticky buds.
- There are many rhymes and rituals to the game of conkers, depending on where you live.

Growing Tips

Plant these relatively hardy trees in moist, well-drained, fertile soil in full sun or partial shade. They are prone to leaf miners, a type of insect that can cause leaves to turn brown and fall early. While they don't damage the tree itself, leaf miners adversely affect its appearance.

Superpower: **Surface Tension**

Lady's mantle

Alchemilla mollis
Native to Romania, Sweden,
Switzerland and the Caucasus

The beauty of this plant only becomes truly apparent after rain. Round droplets of moisture form perfect pearls on the upper surfaces of its velvety, water-resistant leaves – merging into larger pearls to create a glittering effect. The magic is that the droplets are held in position, transforming the whole plant into a bejewelled wonder. The leaves of lady's mantle have hundreds of miniature hairs, which gives them superhydrophobic capabilities. Thus the hairs effectively hold the water droplet above the leaf surfaces, maintaining the surface tension that stops the water draining away and creates perfect droplets seemingly suspended in the air. Humans have been intrigued by these plants' special abilities for decades, and have designed self-drying fabrics inspired by their leaves.

Appearance

Bright lime-green, scalloped leaves cry out to be stroked. Each has 7–11 shallow lobes, creating a pleated effect with fine hairs emerging from the surface. Lady's mantle grows in a mound about 30cm (12in) across and has flowers without petals, which appear as small, light green clusters.

Uses

Its fresh green foliage is perfect for cottage gardens or to soften the hard lines of modern, angular designs. This herbaceous perennial dies back in winter, to resprout again in spring.

Interesting Facts

• Alchemists believed the aquatic pearls on the leaves of lady's mantle were the purest form of water – using them to create their 'elixirs of life' and in experiments attempting to turn base metals into gold. This is why the plant's botanical name shares the alchemist's name, *Alchemilla mollis*. The *mollis* means 'soft', because of the lovely sensation the leaves have when they are touched.

• Its common name, lady's mantle, probably reflects its velvety scalloped leaves, representing the Virgin Mary's coat.

Growing Tips

This is an easy-to-grow plant for your garden, which is unfussy about soil type and will thrive in sun or partial shade. It flowers in midsummer. Trim after flowering to tidy the plant up and encourage new growth – and also to minimize its seeds spreading.

Superpower: **Super Healer**

Garlic

Allium sativum
Native to central Asia to north-eastern Iran

In folklore, garlic acts as a powerful vampire deterrent. But its connection to fictional blood-sucking predators shares a curious connection with its real-life powers of healing associated with the blood. According to the British Heart Foundation, garlic has long been linked with health benefits, from curing colds to lowering blood pressure and cholesterol levels – an antioxidant chemical called allicin is thought to be responsible for its positive effects. Garlic does not stop there as a healer, as it can even help muscles, particularly after a workout. It does this by stimulating testosterone, thus protecting against infection.

Garlic is bursting with vitamins C and B6, manganese and selenium. It even contains vitamins B1 and B5, and calcium, copper and potassium. The chemical diallyl disulfide – an anti-inflammatory – is also found in garlic, which in oil form can be massaged into inflamed muscles or joints for relief. The Arthritis Foundation recommends it to prevent cartilage damage linked to arthritis.

Appearance
The only evidence of anything above the surface when growing garlic is its tall, curling, green stems. Once you unearth the bulbs, you'll have a much better idea of what is going on. Garlic bulbs are white in colour, with a thin, papery layer of skin protecting the cloves. Once you remove this skin, you can separate each clove, like segments of an orange. After removing another tissue-thin layer of skin, either the same shade of white or with hints of a subtle pink, you'll have the waxy cloves ready to cook with.

Uses
Adding garlic to recipes not only introduces more flavour but also many health benefits. Alternatively, you can buy garlic oil for skin and joints, or garlic capsules as a health supplement.

Interesting Facts
• Historically, many cultures have believed in the healing power of garlic, dating back to Ancient Egypt through to Romania, where its powers of protection held it as the superhero plant to protect against evil, which is probably where its connection to Dracula arrived from.
• There are two types of garlic: soft neck and hard neck. Soft is smaller and stores for longer. Hard is larger and has a stronger flavour.
• This member of the onion family was one of the first herbs to be cultivated by humans.

Growing Tips
Garlic grows well in free-draining, weed-free, non-acidic soil, ideally under full sun. Soft-neck types require little maintenance and take up little space, but they do need a period of cold to form a good bulb. Harvest both types in early summer when the leaves turn yellow and droop. Hard-neck varieties store until mid-winter. Garlic can be prone to rust for which there is no control other than removing the diseased plants – and growing in different parts of the garden in successive years to avoid a recurrence.

Superpower: **Rejuvenation and Healing**

Aloe vera

Aloe vera
Native to northern Oman

Aloe vera has been utilized for millennia for its medicinal purposes and anti-ageing properties. Cleopatra was said to have rubbed its sap on her skin and hair daily to keep them soft and lustrous – no wonder the Egyptians called aloe vera the 'eternal plant'. Alexander the Great (who ruled Macedon from 336 to 323 BCE) conquered a whole island just to acquire this plant to treat his wounded soldiers. The Romans also recognized its healing properties, for burns and other skin irritations.

The sap of aloe vera is a clear gel that contains an incredible seventy-five potentially active constituents including vitamins, enzymes, minerals, sugars, lignin, saponins, salicylic acids, amino acids and mucopolysaccharides (which aids in binding moisture to the skin). Aloe vera also supports fibroblast cells that secrete collagen protein to help maintain the structural framework of tissue and keep skin elastic. It's been found to be antiseptic (with six agents that inhibit bacteria, viruses and fungi) and protective of ultraviolet (UV) on the skin.

Appearance
Aloe vera is a succulent, easily grown as a houseplant on a brightly lit windowsill and is striking to look at. Its plump, long-pointed, fleshy leaves of silvery-green form dense clumps, with small, soft-toothed barbs along their sides. Tubular, yellow to orange flowers may appear along spikes in summer.

Uses
It is a soothing balm added to cosmetics, hair conditioners, deodorants, suntan lotions and even to toilet paper, while its moisturizing abilities make it great for sunburn, stretch marks and scars. Aloe vera is also a 'super healer' for inflammation and acne. The gel from aloe vera can be applied directly to your skin. Just cut off a leaf, and wrap clingfilm over the cut point on the plant until it heals. Then squeeze the clear gel from the cut end of the leaf into the palm of your hand or into a bowl. Apply it as liberally as you like.

Interesting Facts
• Aloe has been introduced into the Arabian Peninsula and Africa.
• It is one of the most widely used natural products in the West.
• Aloe plants can survive for over a hundred years.
• The name aloe vera derives from the Arabic word *alloeh* meaning 'shining bitter substance', while *vera* in Latin means 'true'.

Growing Tips
Position aloe vera somewhere warm, sunny and free-draining, where there is little risk of frost. Aloe vera is a particularly low-maintenance houseplant. Plant in a terracotta container (to retain soil temperature) that is free-draining – aloe vera doesn't like to be overwatered. Feed monthly between mid-spring and early autumn with a high-potassium liquid fertilizer. After two or three years, depending on the size of your plant or container, repot your plant to give it a little bit more room to continue to grow.

Superpower: **Mood Changing**

Lemon verbena

Aloysia citrodora
Native to south Bolivia and north-western Argentina

Lemon verbena has the power to change your mood in an instant. Take a leaf and rub it between your fingers then enjoy the zesty, fizzy lemon fragrance. It's like the smelling salts of happiness, and I challenge you not to feel immediately uplifted by this comforting aroma suggestive of traditional childhood sherbet and lemon sweets. It's not just lemon verbena leaves, either. Rub the stem for a fragrant lift, too. Indeed, everything above ground gives off a sensational crisp, fizzy lemon fragrance. The plant's compounds include geraniol, limonene and cineol – naturally present in essential oils and also found in lemon peel. They provide the plant's lemon-like scent.

Appearance

This perennial shrub has long, narrow, delicately toothed leaves, in a light and bright shade of green, growing in bunches of three along the stems. It produces tiny flowers along the ends of the stems in spring, creating a lace-like effect, with white or pale purple blooms appearing opposite one another in short panicles: attractive to look at and a favourite of bees.

Uses

With its textured leaves and delicate flowers, it makes an attractive shrub in a herb garden or mixed flowering border. Leaves can be picked fresh for drinks, for a cheeky addition to summer cocktails or Pimm's. Lemon verbena can also be used in cooking to add lemon flavour to vegetable marinades, fish and poultry dishes, salad dressings, puddings, jams and drinks.

Interesting Facts

- Traditional Iranian medicine used this plant to cure all sorts of ills such as digestive problems, trouble sleeping, colds, fevers and asthma.
- Lemon verbena is a popular plant among children thanks to its sweet scent. reminiscent of lemon sherbet.

Growing Tips

Requires full sun, a sheltered location and well-drained, moisture-retentive soil. It's half-hardy so, if grown outside, will benefit from frost protection and a mulch around the base of the plant, applied in autumn. If grown in a container, bring indoors or place in a heated greenhouse or conservatory during winter. Hard prune in late winter to retain shape and encourage vigorous new growth.

Superpower: **Adapt and Overcome**

Thrift

Armeria maritima
Native to the subarctic and temperate Northern Hemisphere

Thrift is unusual in that it can survive both fresh and saltwater conditions – its Latin name *maritima* pertains to the sea or coast. This compact evergreen perennial even adapts its leaves depending on the level of saline to which it is exposed – thriving in the most hostile of coastal locations including cliff tops, salt marshes, shingle or sandy areas, in shallow, low-nutrient soils. Even when lashed by rainwater one minute, showered with salty sea spray the next, thrift manages environmental conditions that would rapidly kill off most plants. This plant deploys all its resources to survive: for example, its hardy, short-tufted mounds of leaves retain moisture. The common name 'thrift' refers to its propensity to prosper in tough conditions by making small savings wherever possible. When salt levels rise, its leaves produce an amino acid called proline, to prevent foliage damage. If the salt levels become a permanent problem, the plant produces betalain pigments, which help on a longer-term basis.

Appearance

You can spot the bright flowers of thrift around the coast and cliffs between mid-spring and midsummer. It grows in low clumps to protect it from wind damage and sends up long stems supporting pompom-like globes of bright pink, purple, white or red flowers. Its dense, grass-like leaves are evergreen, giving much-needed green colour to shingle beaches around the coast throughout the year.

Uses

This is a perfect plant for a border, wall or rock garden, its beautiful early spring flowers bringing early colour to a garden. It's suitable for container-growing in exposed positions, too.

Interesting Facts

- The stunning flowers give thrift another common name – sea pink.
- Thrift has inspired many artists in paintings, including some that have featured on a series of postage stamps by the Jersey Post for the Royal Mail.
- This plant was featured on the back of the UK threepenny coin between 1937 and 1953, a reminder that frugality was an essential part of everyday life.

Growing Tips

Plant in an alpine trough, scree, rock or gravel garden in well-drained, light soil in full sun, avoiding competition from other plants. Remove the flowering stems before they set seed if you do not want thrift to spread. Thrift is generally hardy and untroubled by pests and diseases.

Plants and the chemical reactions that sustain them are responsible for virtually all life on Earth – providing the oxygen we breathe, the food we eat and the fuel with which we still power the majority of our societies. In fact, it's no exaggeration to say that the act of photosynthesis – the fairly simple process by which plants transform light energy into chemical energy by way of water and carbon dioxide – is the basis of humanity.

Until plant life began to colonize the evolving land masses, some 500 million years ago during the Cambrian Period, humans would not have been able to survive Earth's atmosphere. Temperatures were too high, there was too much carbon dioxide in the atmosphere to sustain life as we know it, and high levels of solar radiation would have killed everything.

The rise of plant life over tens of millions of years stabilized the atmosphere, bringing down carbon dioxide levels by sequestering carbon, which helped regulate the previously hot, wet climate, and created the basic building blocks of life, too. Oxygen produced as a by-product of photosynthesis also formed the ozone layer, between 16km (10 miles) and 32km (20 miles) above the surface of the Earth. Ozone is formed by the action of ultraviolet light on oxygen molecules, but such simplification belies its importance: the ozone layer absorbs some 97 per cent of ultraviolet light and shields us and other living things from the sun's harmful radiation. It also supported the evolution of aerobic respiration – by which we mean breathing.

What happened was, essentially, a greenhouse effect in reverse. As carbon dioxide concentrations fell, so did the Earth's temperature, because less heat from the sun was captured in the lower atmosphere.

This is how the arrival of plant life began the transformation of our planet into the blue-green oasis we see today in photographs taken from space. The global cooling they cleared the way for also helped fuel an explosion of new marine life and, scientists believe, eventually ushered in an ice age that occurred some 445 million years ago.

The earliest plants are likely to have been non-vascular, so-called because they don't have the common systems to carry water internally. In their simplest forms they would have consisted of mosses, liverworts and algaes. These groups are known as bryophytes and are sometimes dismissively called 'lower

Earth's Original Superheroes

plants' in reference to their status as the earliest plant groups to evolve. But they were survivors, and their spread began the transformation of Earth into a habitable planet for complex multicellular life forms such as mammals – providing habitat, food and oxygen.

As well as cooling the atmosphere, plants helped create nutrient cycles and, as recent research suggests, led to the formation of rivers – producing new habitats for the plants and animals that followed in their wake. The evolution of this early plant life on land, into ferns and then, ultimately, forests, moulded the Earth as we know it today – making it unique in the universe as far as we are currently aware.

The great forests of the past – the earliest fossilized remains of which have been dated to around 390 million years ago – were huge carbon sinks, absorbing harmful carbon dioxide from the air and storing it. When they died, the carbon was buried beneath the next layer of growth, and so on, creating huge fossil fuel reserves under our oceans and continents over the course of tens of millions of years. Even with the advent of so-called green energy, this fossilized vegetation still provides as much as 90 per cent of the world's energy. As well

Ocean plankton provides the rest of the oxygen that keeps the Earth habitable and us alive.

as producing some 28 per cent of the world's oxygen, our surviving rainforests absorb around a third of global emissions every year. And when we cut them down or burn them, the carbon they hold gets released back into the atmosphere.

Ocean plankton provides the rest of the oxygen that keeps the Earth habitable and us alive – the average human breathes around 550 litres (123 gallons) of oxygen a day, twice as much as a mature tree can typically produce. Thus, arguably plankton – this most passive of all our neighbours here on Earth – is more responsible for our own existence than any other plant form. So let's hear it for plants.

Superpower: **Can Kill . . . and Cure**

Deadly nightshade

Atropa bella-donna
Native to Europe, through to northern
Iran and north-western Africa

Despite its fearsome reputation as one of the most toxic plants in the eastern hemisphere, nightshade also contributes a powerful counter-nerve agent. This just goes to show that, when it comes to the natural world, you've always got to take the good with the bad. As its botanical name *Atropa* suggests, the foliage and berries contain tropane alkaloids – including atropine, scopolamine and hyoscyamine – that target the nervous system and are extremely dangerous if ingested. Effects include delirium, increased heart rate, blurred vision, hallucinations and, eventually if untreated, death. However, the tropane alkaloids are also used as pharmaceutical anticholinergics, treating a variety of conditions including chronic obstructive pulmonary disease and gastrointestinal disorders, as well as acting as anti-nerve agents, as atropine increases heart rate, countering the nerve agents' ability to slow the heart.

Appearance
Deadly nightshade produces pointed green leaves, with a ribbed appearance, and can grow up to 1m (3ft) in height in bush form. Its flowers are a dark muted purple, tinged yellow-green towards their bases; they hang in slight bell shapes. They eventually die back to develop small, glossy, black berries, grown against the backdrop of five-pointed sepals, looking like a cup framing each berry.

Uses
The best use of deadly nightshade is as a counteragent for the deadly effects of nerve agents but it has a long and storied history in cosmetics, medicine and poison.

Interesting Facts
• The name *bella-donna* comes from *belle* (beautiful) and *donna* (woman), because during the Renaissance ladies would use a refined extract from nightshade to dilute their pupils – a look thought to make them appear more beautiful.
• Deadly nightshade comes from the same family as potatoes (*Solanum tuberosum*; see page 146), tomatoes (*S. lycopersicum*; see page 144), peppers and aubergines.
• The Roman empress Livia Drusilla reputedly used nightshade to poison her husband, Emperor Augustus, while Roman bowmen would dip their arrowheads in the poison.
• In Scotland in the eleventh century, deadly nightshade was used against the invading Anglo-Saxons. Today, soldiers who may be at risk from chemical attack are issued with kits that include extracts of atropine, to counter many nerve agents.

Growing Tips
This herbaceous perennial thrives in most soil types, in full sun or partial shade. As all parts of the plant are toxic, it should be planted at the back of a border and not in a garden where children or animals are present. Flowers should be deadheaded to prevent berries – the most toxic part of the plant – from forming.

Superpower: **Living Barbed Wire**

Berberis

Berberis × stenophylla
The hybrid formula of this artificial cross
is *B. darwinii × B. empetrifolia*

This plant is as hard as nails. It's a beast, growing up to 3m (10ft) tall with long arching branches crammed with spines. When established, it's almost impenetrable – unless you're wearing protective clothing, as the spines can penetrate our skin and tear through the surface. This is why this berberis hybrid makes such a perfect boundary plant if you're concerned about trespassers. In that sense alone, it's a living, growing garden bouncer. The spines on some varieties of *Berberis* are hidden behind the foliage, but *B. × stenophylla* has only small leaves, which offer no protection to the skin and leave you in no doubt about its ability to deter intruders. Yet this plant has a subtle side too – beauty and the beast, if you will – making a graceful, free-standing and impressive flowering mega shrub.

Appearance

Berberis makes an impressive shrub and a great garden feature if planted for aesthetic reasons. Its leaves are leathery and small, pinnate in shape and around 1cm (½in) in size, grouped in clusters above the many thorns. Also, it's evergreen, so it gives year-round colour. It is blessed in mid- and late spring with an abundance of small, ball-like, fragrant flowers in bright yellowy gold. If you plant in a warm, sheltered position, berberis may bear a second flush of flowers in autumn, along with its blue-black berries.

Uses

It can be grown as a very large shrub in a border and is a good back-filler for a large bed. Berberis can also be planted for protective purposes as a dense hedge but requires regular clipping to keep in shape. Being a good coastal plant and particularly low-maintenance, it's ideal for planting on a slope.

Interesting Facts

• This fortress of a shrub has another interesting side. Its spines and density make it a perfect protector of little birds, and an ideal nesting site, as cats and other predators cannot enter.

• Its berries provide an autumn food source, while the spring flowers supply meals for insects during hatching time.

Growing Tips

Berberis performs well in most soil types but does not like to be waterlogged. It's especially vigorous in full sun or partial shade. Water it well in its first year on dry days, to allow it to establish. Just ensure you prune it back when necessary, as this plant is a fast and efficient grower. When mature, berberis is an incredibly low-maintenance, tough plant that pretty much looks after itself.

Superpower: **Call of the Butterflies**

Butterfly bush

Buddleja davidii
Native to central and south-eastern China

A flight of butterflies is known as a kaleidoscope because of the fabulous display of cryptic colouration, and there are few better places to enjoy one of nature's most glorious sights than around a *Buddleja* on a sunny summer's day. Known as the 'butterfly bush', the sheer volume of butterflies it attracts to its flowers is a sight to behold. Its secret is in its flowers. Each is in fact a panicle, a branched cluster of many hundreds of tiny individual blooms filled with sweet nectar, containing the sucrose, glucose and fructose needed to keep its aerial visitors aloft.

Appearance

Butterfly bushes are alive with colour between early summer and mid-autumn, both in terms of their flowering panicles and their visitors. Flowers aside, these bushes are evergreen so you can enjoy their soft-green foliage throughout the year. Some varieties have variegated leaves, with lighter creamy shades around the edges and a refreshing sage-green at the centre, while others boast delicate shades of green across their smooth, spearhead-shaped leaves.

Uses

Combining the sheer volume of flowers with the high quality of its nectar, a single butterfly bush provides a delicious all-you-can-eat buffet for butterflies, and is the perfect reason to attract these spectacularly beautiful winged insects to your garden. Choose varieties with blue, red, purple or pink flowers to attract maximum butterflies. The insects' vision spectrum favours ultraviolet (UV), but they can also perceive red wavelength colours. Therefore, white or pale flowers are less attractive. And not just butterflies either; this plant attracts myriad airborne insects, too.

Interesting Facts

• First introduced from China in the 1890s.
• Their double-winged seeds can fly, meaning the shrub spreads fast and far. Indeed, it's classed as an invasive species.
• During the 1950s, empty bomb sites in Britain became a flourish of colour as the butterfly bush's extraordinary ability to grow in the most impossible places brought wastelands to life. They can still be seen in unused spaces, alongside railways and in (and sometimes on) disused industrial buildings.
• The cross-section of a butterfly bush's branches are square rather than round.

Growing Tips

Butterfly bush grows almost anywhere but for the best results in your garden choose a sheltered spot with full sun to encourage the nectar-rich flowers. Give a potassium fertilizer in spring, to encourage flowering, and deadhead frequently throughout the season. Cut the whole plant back hard in mid- or late spring, to keep its growth in check; remove dead wood and shape it. If ignored, this shrub can grow huge and sprawling. Butterfly bushes might be stunning but don't underestimate their determination.

Superpower: **Good Luck and Protection**

White heather

Calluna vulgaris
Native to Macaronesia, Europe to central Siberia and northern Morocco

White heather has long been associated with good luck and just a sprig of it is thought to bring positive fortune to an individual. Not so long ago, vendors would go door-to-door selling sprigs for luck. The tradition is heard of in Ireland, but seems to stem from Scotland; there are many recordings of the magical luck provided by white heather. In 1544 in the Battle of the Shirts, Clan Macdonald of Clan Ranald and Clan Cameron accredited their victory over the men of Clan Fraser to wearing white heather in their bonnets. Some accounts claim that in 1746, after the Jacobite rebellion was crushed by British forces at the Battle of Culloden, Ewen MacPherson of Cluny, known as 'Cluny Macpherson', evaded capture by sleeping on a patch of white heather. As John Brown, Queen Victoria's favourite attendant, apparently told Her Majesty, no true Highlander would pass by a patch without picking a sprig.

Other folklore confers magic qualities on this plant, including the belief that it grows over the final resting place of fairies. Another is that white heather will only grow in a spot where no blood has fallen on a battlefield. Some attribute its status to its relative rarity; others to its medicinal benefits or its importance to beneficial insects including bees.

Appearance

Calluna vulgaris are dense, woody, evergreen shrubs, which carpet the ground and are typically found dusting the highlands of Scotland. The plant's spikes are coated in tiny, scale-like leaves, from which the bell-shaped flowers hang, offering consistent colour throughout the plant. White heather is a variety in the *Calluna* genus, but other genera include *Erica*, identifiable by its needle-shaped foliage, and *Daboecia*, with leaves that are more oval or lance-shaped.

Uses

You can pick heather and wrap it with a ribbon to be worn as a buttonhole or a posy. Add a sprig to a wedding bouquet, or place on the table for guests to enjoy. And hang a garland in a new home for good fortune and protection.

Interesting Facts

• Heather has traditionally been sourced for fuel, building materials, bedding and thatch.
• It was also used to make brooms, which explains its Latin name – *Callunais* – derived from the Greek word meaning 'to brush'.

Growing Tips

The shrub's nectar-rich flowers attract bees and flower from midsummer into the autumn, although some cultivars flower in winter depending on the conditions, and will provide food at a time of year when sources of nectar are in short supply. Heather needs watering regularly during the first year of planting, and prefers acidic soil; once established, it is drought tolerant. Prune lightly immediately after flowering to stop it becoming too woody, but do not cut into old wood as it will not regenerate. The majority of heather varieties are hardy, whilst all *Calluna* varieties are fully hardy and trouble-free.

Superpower: **Power of Heat**

Chillies

Capsicum
Native from Mexico to tropical America

These fiery fruits – they are related to tomatoes (see page 144), potatoes (see page 146) and aubergines, and not considered vegetables – contain the compound capsaicin (pronounced cap-say-sin), which binds to receptors in the lining of your mouth causing a burning sensation. The pain releases the body's natural painkillers, endorphins, which also give a feeling of happiness; one of the attractions of hot foods. Capsaicin is found in the seeds of the chilli, but more commonly in the 'placenta' – the spongy white membrane in which the seeds are embedded. The pungency of chillies is measured in Scovilles, a test created in 1912 which calculates the progressive dilution rate chillies need to become free of heat. A fairly hot chilli is about 3,000 Scoville heat units, while the hottest chilli on record, the 'Carolina Reaper', boasts a measure of two million Scovilles – more powerful than pepper spray used by law enforcement.

Appearance
These spicy fruits vary considerably in appearance, thanks to the many different varieties now cultivated globally. The plants however all produce tall stems, with spearhead-shaped, smooth leaves. Their lovely white flowers are followed by fruits in late summer. The fruit themselves vary in colour depending on ripeness, but the classic shape is long, thin, slightly curved and pepper-like. Some varieties have been grown to be much shorter and rounder – the bell-shaped 'Scotch Bonnet', for example – while others are somewhere in between.

Uses
Used widely in cooking, most famously in Asian dishes, the heat created from chillies ranges from subtle warmth to intense burning. You can harvest chillies at different stages of ripening – green being young, then orange turning to red. Pick fresh to cook with immediately; they can also be frozen or dried for use later.

Interesting Facts
• The heat from eating chillies impacts only mammals – birds are completely unaffected.
• Chillies have been eaten in Mexico as far back as 7000 BCE.
• Early Mayans, Aztecs and Incas used chillies as currency.
• Chillies have antioxidant and anti-inflammatory properties, vitamin C and bioactive compounds.

Growing Tips
Growing your own chillies from seed is easy, and they are ideal for growing in small pots on a windowsill or in a large container in a greenhouse. Water regularly but sparingly in the growing season, leaving compost slightly dry as a slightly stressed plant will encourage hotter fruit. Pinch out the tops of the first flowering shoots to encourage more branching and greater fruit production. Feed weekly after the first fruit sets with a high-potassium tomato fertilizer. Adding a mulch of organic matter around the base of the plant will help keep in moisture. If growing indoors, open windows to allow pollinating insects access to the flowers to ensure a good fruit set. Alternatively, hand pollinate by dabbing the centre of each flower with a narrow artist's paintbrush. Harvest regularly to encourage the plant to produce more fruit.

Superpower: **Feline Repellent**

Scaredy cat plant

Coleus caninus
Native from Sudan to southern Africa, and India to Myanmar

While there are many noble plant superpowers, scaredy cat plant does not boast one of them. It's a horticultural honker, one of the most horrid-smelling plants you can grow – its scent is reputed to even deter cats and other mammals including dogs, rabbits and foxes. So while it's not unpleasant to look at – lush green leaves support striking purple flowers – this tender perennial is most useful as a non-harmful deterrent to neighbouring cats who might be using your borders or vegetable patch as their toilet. The good news is that the scent of scaredy cat plant is activated only by physical contact, such as treading on or brushing against it. Bruising its leaves releases a pungent odour that will make you recoil, and its sap remains on your hands so wear gloves if handling. And avoid planting near your patio or barbecue area.

Appearance

The unpleasantly scented, grey-green leaves of scaredy cat plant are rounded and scalloped, and grow opposite one another on the stems. Lavender-like flowers are produced between early and late summer in delicate purple shades on stalks that reach up and through the foliage, for an attention-grabbing feature.

Uses

Plant as a scented deterrent where you are getting unwanted garden visitors. A bonus is that the smell may discourage unwanted locals from sitting on your front wall or taking a shortcut through your garden.

Interesting Facts

• The botanical name comes from the Greek words *koleus* (sheath), which refers to the plant's enclosed stamens, and *caninus* (dogs).

Growing Tips

Scaredy cat plant is easy to grow but not reliably hardy, so in frost-prone areas plant in a container so that it can be brought under cover before the first frosts. It requires little maintenance other than gentle pruning to shape (remember those gloves). It is drought-tolerant once established.

Superpower: **Beautiful but Deadly**

Lily of the valley

Convallaria majalis
Native from Europe to the Caucasus (with the exemption of north-west European Russia)

Lily of the valley is a beautiful woodland flower associated with purity, humility and good luck, yet it's also deadly. Every single part of the plant is poisonous, from its flowers and stems to its leaves. The highest concentration of toxins – a form of cardenolide or steroid – are in its roots. Eating them can induce intoxication, palpitations, dizziness, heart fibrillations and potentially death. Cats are especially sensitive to lily of the valley, eating as little as two leaves can cause kidney failure and even kill them. Despite this, it's a popular cut flower, sold alone or in mixed bouquets.

So why is lily of the valley so revered? Probably thanks to its beauty, making this herbaceous perennial a staple of wedding bouquets. In Germany, it is associated with the virgin goddess Ostara. The Victorians saw lily of the valley as signifying a return to happiness and innocence.

Appearance

In late spring, dainty, bell-shaped, pendent flowers appear like droplets along the bottom edge of the stem, hanging down and swaying in the breeze. Vibrant green leaves provide a luscious backdrop to these pink or white blooms, ensuring they stand out against the woodland floor or other garden plants.

Uses

The lily of the valley is a beautiful plant when grown under trees and is known as an indicator to demarcate ancient woodland habitats. It is sold in garden centres to bring colour not only to a border but also to a container. Florists use the plant widely for its visual beauty and perfumed fragrance.

Interesting Facts

- The rock group Queen has a ballad, 'Lily of the Valley', on their third album, *Sheer Heart Attack*, released in 1974.
- The second part of the botanical name of this plant is *majalis*, which means 'belonging to May'.

Growing Tips

Plant in fertile, moist soil in full or partial shade. Do not let plants dry out as they may not recover. Once established, plants require little or no maintenance.

Superpower: **Razor-Sharp**

Pampas grass

Cortaderia selloana, aka *C. argentea*
Native from Bolivia to southern South America

The leaves of pampas grass have adapted over time to protect themselves from predators by producing vicious slicing edges sharp enough to cut paper, and capable of causing superficial wounds to humans and other unwary animals. Their edges also have tooth-like edging, which inflicts razor penetration. As a result, this invasive flowering plant is not suitable for areas with children or pets, and you're well advised to wear thick leather gauntlet gloves when handling it. Its defensive mechanism is all the more surprising, given that when the pampas is in flower the plumes look so soft and gentle, belying the fact that there are hundreds and hundreds of whip-like leaf blades beneath them. In part because of this, the old way of trimming the plant after flowering was to set it on fire, burning it back. But is it no longer done, as it risks destroying habitats, and burning it can damage the crown of the plant.

Appearance
Pampas is an elegant, grass-like plant with large arching foliage, which appears in a spray from the ground. In summer, its great feathery plumes of flowers stand tall above the main body of the plant, moving gracefully in the breeze like ostrich feathers. There are ivory-white varieties and a pink one too. Pampas grass is a large plant, easily growing up to 3m (10ft) in height, with a generous spread in the appropriate conditions.

Uses
The flowers of this impressive plant can be dried for indoor decoration. A great lawn-statement plant, it offers shelter for some garden creatures. Pampas was also often used as a hibernation haven for garden creatures and tortoises before going out of fashion at the end of the 1980s.

Interesting Facts
• It's said that sales of this once hugely popular plant fell because of the the bizarre urban myth that its planting suggested the home owners were 'swingers'. No matter how strange, the association was so strong that sales of pampas grass plummeted and its popularity rapidly dwindled.
• Today pampas grass is making a big comeback, in large part thanks to interior designers using the long-lasting spectacular plumes as dried flowers.

Growing Tips
Position in a sunny site, with moist, well-drained soil; avoid unsheltered spots vulnerable to strong winds, as this will bend and potentially break pampas grass stalks. Give the plant plenty of space to spread, as it's big. It's tough too, deer-resistant and trouble-free from pests and diseases. Pampas grass is incredibly low-maintenance when established; just remove the old flower plumes when they start to fall.

Plants really are nature's superheroes. Not only have they made the Earth habitable by lowering temperatures, stabilizing the climate and producing the very oxygen we breathe, but they are the foundation for all our food, too. They provide the nutrients, vitamins, minerals, fibre and water that our bodies need to survive, while forming the basis of nourishing all the other species we eat. The meat and dairy products that we consume are largely produced by farmed animals fed on plants – which means that, even when we're eating meat, indirectly we're consuming calories created by plants. As a result, everything we eat is fundamentally derived from photosynthesis combining the sun's energy with carbon dioxide and water to create energy in the form of sugars, which form the basis of the complex carbon molecules that nourish us.

Think of it this way: among multicellular organisms, only plants have the ability to convert sunlight into organic substances via photosynthesis. Because of this, plants are the planet's primary producers on which all other living organisms depend to some extent or other. Without them, there would be almost no other life. So we should be grateful the planet has an estimated 400,000 species of plants, all playing a role in supporting life as we know it, while also providing us with vegetables, fruits, seeds, oils, beverages, spices, essences and other edible products.

Typically, plants make up around a fifth of our food, unless we're vegetarian or vegan, and a staggering 60 per cent of the plants we eat come from just twelve individual species: wheat, sugar cane, sweetcorn, soy, potatoes, palm oil, cassava, sorghum, millet, groundnuts, sweet potatoes and rice. If you cut out plants, you'd immediately lose all the fibre in your diet as well as a multitude of other vitamins and minerals.

Fibre is essentially the intact and largely indigestible carbohydrates from the cell walls of plants, and it's crucial to human digestive systems. Unlike sugars and starches, it passes undigested through the small intestine and into the large intestine. While other food components such as fats, proteins and carbs are broken down and absorbed into the blood, which carries them to where they are needed, fibre passes out of your body as a waste product. But it's a vital one, increasing the weight and size of your stool by absorbing water and softening it, allowing it to pass smoothly through your digestive system without

Plants as Food

getting stuck, and thus maintaining bowel health.

Studies have shown that increased dietary fibre is linked to lower risks of cardiovascular disease, diabetes and colorectal cancer in humans – so eat more plants to stay healthy. To lower the risk of serious health problems like heart disease, strokes and some cancers, the World Health Organization recommends a minimum of 400g (14oz) of fruit and vegetables a day – commonly shortened to five-a-day, each portion of fruit and vegetables being 80g (2¾oz).

Research by the American Gut Project, a crowd-sourced study involving more than 10,000 participants, suggests however that we should try and consume thirty different varieties a week for a healthy, varied diet and a diverse gut biome. The magic number thirty was the tipping point researchers found made the most marked difference to participants' health. The diet works like this: a point is given for every 'new' plant you eat in a given week, and by including thirty different plant-based foods you're covering the broadest spectrum of nutrients that you need to keep your body, and especially your gut, healthy. If this sounds arduous, remember it doesn't just include fruits and vegetables but wholegrains, nuts, seeds, herbs and spices as well. You also need to bear in mind that not all plant-derived foods are worth a point. Processed foods like pasta, white bread and white rice, made from the inner part of the wheat grain from which the fibre-rich bran has been stripped, don't count.

So keep an eye on your intake of plants and try to hit the magic thirty every week.

Studies have shown that increased dietary fibre is linked to lower risks of cardiovascular disease, diabetes and colorectal cancer in humans – so eat more plants to stay healthy.

Superpower: **Good Luck and Fortune**

Money tree

Crassula ovata, aka *C. argentea*
Native from south-eastern Mozambique to
south-eastern Cape Provinces

The money tree is renowned across many Asian cultures for attracting luck and wealth. You'll find these compact houseplants in restaurants, takeaways and offices, often by the entrance to help usher in and maintain prosperity. Also known as the jade plant, friendship plant or lucky plant, there's an Asian saying: 'Jade by the door, poor no more'. According to tradition, the money tree will both aid and benefit its owner depending on the plant's position in the home or office: east locations benefit health, scholarly pursuits and family harmony; south-east ones promote wealth; west locations encourage luck for children; and north-west invites luck for mentors, teachers and helpful people. There is also the belief that this plant also aids mental well-being in its given property, as it nourishes chi, the uplifting force said to bring light and energy. While these reactions are down to human faith rather than scientific processes, there are few plants that boast quite so many potential benefits when it comes to luck, fortune and happiness as the money tree.

Appearance

With its chunky, trunk-like branches and glossy green leaves, the money tree most closely resembles a bonsai. The wedge-shaped foliage of this succulent is plump and water-filled. In the right conditions, it will produce little clusters of small, fragrant, star-shaped flowers.

Uses

In frost-prone areas, it's commonly grown as an indoor plant, tolerant of neglect and ideal for low-maintenance situations like holiday homes or rentals. It can be moved outside onto a patio or balcony during summer but must be protected from heavy rain.

Interesting Facts

• The money tree can root from a single leaf in water. Pot cuttings and give to family or friends for a living reminder of your relationship.
• These hardy little plants can easily reach seventy years of age.

Growing Tips

Grow in peat-free, cacti and succulent compost and position on a brightly lit windowsill or desk (not directly in the midday sun). This plant will warn you if it's getting too much sunlight, its leaves taking a red tinge at their tips. This isn't harmful to the plant, but if you want to reduce the redness move your money tree to a slightly shadier spot. Water little and often during summer, and less regularly in winter, the greatest killer of money trees being over-watering. Repot it in a bigger container every two years. These grow slowly but, with patience, they ultimately reach up to 2m (7ft) in height, making a striking feature. In the wild it can propagate itself with fallen branches, which root themselves to form new plants.

Superpower: **Cool as a . . .**

Cucumber

Cucumis sativus
Native to the Himalayas, north Thailand
and southern China

The cucumber has a very special trait. For thousands of years, it has been used as a natural coolant for the palate or face. Because it is up to 96 per cent water, the inner temperature of a cucumber can be as much as 20 degrees cooler than the ambient temperature. Its rubbery green skin also acts as an insulator for the contents. This is where the term 'as cool as a cucumber' comes from. Cultivated by humans for more than 3,000 years and believed to originate somewhere between the Bay of Bengal and the Himalayas, this fruit is bursting with cool contents – water to hydrate, potassium to help blood pressure, fibre for a balanced cholesterol level – and both the inside and the nutrient-packed skin give a good daily dose of many major vitamins: B1, B2, B3, B5, B6, C, folic acid, calcium, iron, zinc, magnesium and phosphorus. The main flavour of the cucumber originates in its seeds, and a half cup of them contains just ten calories, has no fat or protein and just 2g (¹⁄₁₄oz) of carbohydrates.

Appearance

The plant produces large, triangular and slightly lobed leaves and both male and female flowers. The fruit grows long and cylindrical, though the length, thickness and symmetry can vary. The texture of the fruit skin can also differ, with some fruits being perfectly smooth while others have a slightly spikier appearance. The skin colour varies from a lighter green to darker shades, or a combination of the two. Cucumber plants, being members of the gourd family, are climbers or scramblers, so these fruits are produced periodically along the plant's vines.

Uses

Cucumber sandwiches go right back to nineteenth-century India, where British army officers would eat them in the teahouses, along with afternoon tea, to keep them cool. Today, the tradition of cucumber sandwiches lives on at society events and garden parties. Cucumbers are used widely in salads or as an ingredient in cold soups and are, of course, an essential embellishment to summer drinks like Pimm's.

Interesting Facts

- The Roman emperor Tiberius had cucumbers served to him every day; his gardeners even forced them to fruit out of season, to please their master.
- Charlemagne, whose empire spanned Europe during the Early Middle Ages, reputedly had cucumbers grown.
- Cucumbers were said to have been introduced to England in the fourteenth century, lost for two centuries and then reintroduced.

Growing Tips

Varieties exist for growing indoors and outdoors, but never must they mix, or they will cross-pollinate and produce bitter, seed-filled fruits. Indoor cucumbers need lots of heat and don't require pollinating. Increase humidity in the greenhouse by regularly spraying the floor with water. Outdoor cucumbers tolerate lower temperatures, and need to be insect-pollinated; water them regularly.

Feed all cucumber plants weekly with a high-potassium fertilizer once flowers appear. Pinch out the growing tips when the plant reaches the top of its support. Also, remove the tip of each flowering sideshoot once fruits have started to develop.

Plants are prone to cucumber mosaic virus, powdery mildew, whitefly and red spider mites.

Superpower: **Living Beads**

String-of-pearls

Curio rowleyanus
Native to the Cape Provinces of South Africa

This incredible flowering plant of the daisy family – taking the form of a perennial succulent vine – grows in creeping beads of grape-like foliage across the arid earth of its natural South African environment. Stems trail over the ground, rooting where they touch and forming dense, mat-like clusters. Its leaves are spherical and initially resemble the garden pea before growing into a grape-like form. The spherical leaf shape has evolved over time in response to the arid, desert-like conditions in which string-of-pearls thrives; it reduces water loss by decreasing its surface area as much as possible. The loss of surface area is compensated by this smart little plant using a clever trick when it comes to photosynthesis, needed to produce food: an epidermal, crescent-shaped window on one side of each leaf allows sunlight inside to increase the area available for food production. However, be warned: the foliage of string-of-pearls, also known as string-of-beads, is toxic to humans and will cause vomiting and diarrhoea.

Appearance
String-of-pearls is a frost-tender, sprawling succulent, which trails across the ground or tumbles over the edge of a plant pot, creating a softening and refreshing look. In the right conditions, this dainty succulent will produce small, cinnamon-scented, white flowers, which look like little fireworks.

Uses
String-of-pearls makes a most lively and fascinating houseplant when grown in a container or hanging pot, trailing its leaves, creating a stylish feature.

Interesting Facts
• The name *Curio* translates to 'curiosity', the plant named so because of its unusual appearance.

Growing Tips
Grow in cactus compost in a bright spot out of direct sunlight. Water only when compost dries out, as it stores water in its 'pearl' leaves; water especially sparingly in winter. Place the pot in a saucer of water for around half an hour; do not water the plant from above. Feed with half-strength liquid feed monthly between mid-spring and early autumn. Repot when needed in spring.

Superpower: **Spontaneous Combustion**

Gas plant

Dictamnus albus
Native from Europe to south-western Siberia and the western Himalayas

The gas plant isn't known colloquially as the burning bush for nothing. On hot windless days, this ornamental flowering plant will burst into flames in a flash if it comes into contact with a source of ignition – and sometimes without even needing one. The flames are fed by naturally occurring, volatile oils from its flowers which, once ignited, swiftly burn themselves out leaving the plant largely unharmed. It's a fascinating piece of garden chemistry. The plant's oils decompose into a naturally flammable compound called chavicol, a type of phenylpropene, a flammable liquid or vapour. In the absence of a breeze, this can build up around the plant, creating the conditions for ignition when a flashpoint is triggered either by high temperatures or, more commonly, a spark. It's believed gas plant primarily produces these chemicals as an unpleasant scent to deter insects, rather than for reasons of combustion, but both would have a deterrent effect if you were a greenfly.

Appearance
Gas plant's flowers grow upwards on tall spires, reaching to 90cm (36in) tall with a spread of 60cm (24in). Its blooms are typically pink or white, and grow on racemes, creating vivid columns. Each flower has five petals, giving them an almost orchid-like appearance. Pink blooms are particularly striking, as they have darker pink veining through the petals. The foliage is a vibrant shade of green, growing in smooth pointed formations opposite one another on the stems, creating a luscious base from which the flowers emerge. Typically, the foliage smells of lemons.

Uses
This fully hardy plant is primarily a beautiful flowering border favourite, planted to provide summer colour.

Interesting Facts
• Gas plant was also known for its smelly seedpods, an old name for the plant being *Tragium* (from the Greek word *tragos*, which means 'goat'). This was because people thought this name best represented the gas plant's fragrance.

Growing Tips
Plant in light, alkaline, moderately fertile, well-drained soil in full sun or partial shade. Don't position too near to your house or other sources of possible ignition or fuel.

Superpower: **Takes Your Voice**

Dumb cane

Dieffenbachia
Native from Mexico to subtropical America

The dumb cane gets its name because it can quite literally stop you talking if ingested – not that it's a good idea to try. Chewing and eating this plant causes temporary paralysis of the vocal cords, tongue, mouth and throat. And if you were to rub the sap into your eyes, and you absolutely must not, it can even lead to temporary blindness and swelling of the eyelids. This is because dumb cane leaves and stems contain proteolytic enzymes and needle-like calcium oxalate crystals as a defence mechanism – effectively dissuading animals from eating them. But beware, given its toxic properties, dumb cane should not be trimmed without gloves, nor is it advisable to grow it where there are young children or pets. Make sure to wash your hands after handling.

Appearance
The oval variegated leaves are simple and smooth, curving over from a long central stem. Typically lighter at the centre, the leaves get richer in colour towards their edges. These frost-tender plants will rarely bloom when grown as houseplants, but in their native environment can produce flowers on a spadix – a fleshy stem – quite similar in appearance to those of the peace lily (*Spathiphyllum*; see page 148).

Uses
The dumb cane is a good indoor air purifier, particularly for removing xylene (a sweet-smelling hydrocarbon) caused by paints, printers, polishes and solvents from the air. A build-up of xylene can cause headaches, nausea and head fog.

Interesting Facts
• This plant was one of the first to reach Europe during the Austro-Brazilian expeditions in the early 1800s.
• In the Amazon, dumb cane's sap was traditionally used to poison arrowheads.

Growing Tips
Grow in bright indirect light or partial shade but out of direct sun and draughts, in steady temperatures of 18–24°C (65–75°F). Rotate the plant often, to keep it growing evenly. Mist leaves regularly or keep the pot on a tray of moist pebbles; water when the compost is slightly dry in the top layer (sparingly in winter). Feed monthly with a weak liquid fertilizer. Repot when dumb cane becomes root-bound. Prune to avoid it becoming leggy. Dumb cane may be affected by mealybugs and scale insects. Both usually occur on the underside of leaves; remove with a damp cloth. Fine webbing on mottled leaves may indicate spider mites. If so, increase humidity by misting more regularly and spraying affected leaves with a plant oil or fatty acid product.

Superpower: **Counting**

Venus flytrap

Dionaea muscipula
Native from eastern North Carolina to
eastern South Carolina

This plant's superpowers are astonishing – it can count and it also employs a simple form of memory. These give the Venus flytrap a crude understanding of the concept of time – something unique in the plant world. Evolving from simpler carnivorous plants, which lived on Earth 65 million years ago, this horticultural wonder has adapted into an efficient predator. It not only traps flies for food, but has also devised a system to identify whether what falls into its trap is a fly or a small leaf, by evaluating movement. Inside the flytrap's leaves are numerous sensory hairs. If one of them is touched, the plant is alerted and this starts a calcium countdown inside. But unless another hair is touched within around 30 seconds, the plant decides it was a false alarm and resets itself. However, if another hair is touched within that 30-second window, the plant releases another burst of calcium, the trap closes on the fly, and its digestive enzymes get to work on its prey.

Appearance
This is a striking, low-growing, frost-tender plant with two-lobed leaves disguising intriguing traps. The outside of the trap is green, while its inside is deep red, meat-coloured crimson, to attract insects. Venus flytrap bears white, five-petalled flowers on tall stalks.

Uses
When placed on the kitchen windowsill in summer, Venus flytrap will serve as an organic fly catcher. You'll find yourself checking each day if it has caught anything – even willing the fly on the window to go near your plant – or swatting a fly and feeding your plant yourself. Most rewarding.

Interesting Facts
• There are lots of carnivorous plants, all with different ways to trap flies. One, pitcher plant (*Sarracenia*), uses a tall, narrow trap, tempting flies down it with the promise of nectar, but inside the trap are downward-pointing hairs stopping the fly from climbing out, and the bottom contains digestive enzymes. The sundew plant (*Drosera*) also has sticky elements, where flies get stuck and then digested.

Growing Tips
The plant needs to be constantly moist, so sit it in a saucer of water, specifically rainwater, and position it in a brightly lit spot. However, Venus flytrap can tolerate partial shade. Best positioned in a humid room, like your bathroom or kitchen, misting regularly with distilled or rainwater. To boost the energy of the plant so it develops more vegetative growth and traps, snip off the flowers as soon as they start to form.

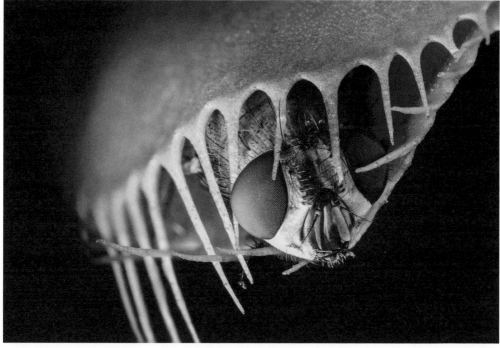

Superpower: **Accelerated Growth**

Mile-a-minute

Fallopia baldschuanica
Native from Tadzhikistan and eastern Afghanistan to western Pakistan

As its fabulous common name implies, the mile-a-minute plant grows exceedingly fast – by as much as a staggering 15cm (6in) a day under optimum conditions. Over a single growing season, this flowering variety of the knotweed family can, if unchecked, climb up to 50m (165ft) – the equivalent of two, two-storey houses stacked on top of one another. It's been suggested the human eye can even see it growing. I'm not so sure of that, but it might have been one of the inspirations behind the classic children's story, *Jack and the Beanstalk*. Beware though if you plant this species; it is invasive and aggressive and, if not kept in trim, will soon grow wildly out of control. It spreads rapidly via its roots, seeds and rhizomes (or underground stems), and can easily grow roots from a cutting. It's so tough that it's even pest-proof – scientists have discovered that it produces its own greenfly repellent.

Appearance
This rambling vine has long twisting stems, soft at the tip and reddish-green in colour, and woody at the base. Its bright green leaves are 4–10cm (1½–4in) long, and shaped like an arrowhead. Small, white-tinged, pink flowers on a drooping cluster emerge all over the plant, changing it from a massive, tangled, sprawling clump into a beautiful cloud of white. The flowers are also wonderfully scented. In autumn, the leaves fall to show a framework of twisted branches.

Uses
Without a doubt, mile-a-minute plant is ideal when it comes to covering a garden eyesore. From oil tanks and old sheds to ugly walls or fences, you name it, this plant will disguise it.

Interesting Fact
• Mile-a-minute has several other common names including Russian vine, silver lace vine and the fleeceflower, in reference to its stunning floral display.

Growing Tips
Mile-a-minute plants as we've already established are extremely fast and successful growers. If you choose to grow it at home, you can rest assured that you won't have to do much more than control where it goes. Choose a spot with poor but well-drained soil in full sun or partial shade, where there is a strong structure that can take the weight of a heavy plant. Attempt to keep it away from other plants or you'll risk them being smothered. Carry out regular and liberal pruning.

While plants are self-evidently a source of food and shelter, their role as a source of medicine remains underappreciated by some people. However, medicinal plants have been used for healing since the beginning of our civilization, certainly before we developed the skills to write down our discoveries. Ancient races harvested seeds, herbs, leaves, fruit and bark to treat a variety of illnesses with greater or lesser success. Traditional Chinese herbal medicine dates back thousands of years, while the oldest discovered text describing the use of plant products as medicine was found in a Sumerian clay slab from Nagpur, India, and written approximately 5,000 years ago. It contains information about using poppy (*Papaver*), henbane (*Hyoscyamus niger*) and mandrake (*Mandragora officinarum*) as therapeutics – all three are powerful narcotics providing pain relief, sedation and calming.

The Amazon rainforest is the most abundant greenhouse on the planet, home to more than 80,000 known plant species and countless more that are yet to be discovered; it is also known by scientists and the pharmacological industry as the world's largest medicine cabinet. An astonishing quarter of all drugs and medicines used today are derived from plants of the rainforest and around 11 per cent of the drugs considered essential by the World Health Organization originated in flowering plants. Thanks to decades of research, we're able to harness the lifesaving powers of superhero plants whose chemical compounds form the basis of powerful drugs that can help combat and alleviate everything from cancer to Parkinson's disease and malaria. And even when modern drugs aren't directly made using plants, they have often inspired thousands of synthetic medicines over the past few decades, many of which are now used as frontline treatments for everything from cancer to heart disease. A perfect example is the humble aspirin, today one of the most widely used drugs in the world. It is derived from the bark of a willow (*Salix*, see page 130).

The medicinal effect of plants isn't merely related to popping a pill. Simple exposure to the great outdoors – most effectively woods and forests – has been shown to boost our immune systems. While breathing in fresh air, we also inhale phytoncides – airborne chemicals that trees and plants give off to protect themselves from insects. Phytoncides

Plants as Medicine

An astonishing quarter of all drugs and medicines used today are derived from plants of the rainforest and around 11 per cent of the drugs considered essential by the World Health Organization originated in flowering plants.

have antibacterial and antifungal qualities, which, scientists have shown, help plants fight disease.

When we breathe in these helpful compounds, we respond by increasing the number and activity of the white blood cells that combat infections in our bodies – thus boosting our immune systems. One study suggested the positive impact of a three-day forest trip lasted for more than a month. Not only that but it's widely recognized that spending time in the natural world and especially near trees boosts our well-being and reduces stress.

Exercising outdoors among trees, or simply relaxing amid that natural environment, reduces stress and lowers blood pressure, according to numerous studies. Even looking at pictures of trees has a similar, though less dramatic, effect. And urban gardens, parks and green spaces have all been shown to produce similarly positive effects.

So spend some time in nature for your physical and mental health.

Superpower: **Anti-Freeze**

Snowdrop

Galanthus nivalis
Native from the Pyrenees to Ukraine

This tough little plant flowers at the very start of the year during the cold, dark winter months – bringing us joy at the sight of its beautiful, nodding, pearl-white flowers and a foretaste of the spring to come. Snowdrops can do this because of their superpower. After all, hard winter soils and brutal frosts are not ideal conditions for flowering bulbs. But the snowdrop is no ordinary bulb. First off, its leaf tips are sharpened to help it break through the cold, hard soil. In France, they call snowdrops *perce-neige* (snow piercer). While other plants freeze, burst and die in sub-zero temperatures, the snowdrop thrives, as it contains proteins that perform an anti-freeze function in its cells. This superpower inhibits ice crystals from forming, protecting snowdrops from frost. It doesn't end there either. To spread their seeds, snowdrops enlist the largest army known to nature – ants. Each seed has a small, oil- and protein-rich appendage called an elastiome. These attract ants, which collect the seeds and carry them to their underground nests to feed the elastiome to their larvae. The seeds themselves remain untouched, effectively planted by the ants.

Appearance

Being one of the few plants to flower so early in the year, snowdrops inevitably stand out amid the late winter gloom. Their striking, bell-shaped blooms hang downwards from refreshingly bright green stems. Depending on the variety, their flowers are either enclosed cup shapes, or slightly more open, featuring green details on the edges of the inner petals.

Uses

Snowdrops are perfect for a border, tub, under a tree or in a rock garden, to provide early colour. They're a marvellous plant for pollinators when food is scarce, as other plants are yet to wake from their winter slumber.

Interesting Facts

• Snowdrops are poisonous due to lycorine and galantamine – alkaloid compounds that are particularly concentrated in their bulbs, and also found in daffodils (*Narcissus*). Ingesting bulbs can lead to diarrhoea and vomiting. Galantamine is of particular interest in combating Alzheimer's Disease; when synthetically produced, it helps preserve the chemical messenger acetylcholine, lower levels of which have been linked to the disease in the brains of patients.
• Snowdrops are not named after snow; they are named after earrings.
• The Greek name *Galanthus* means 'milk flower'.

Growing Tips

Although bulbs can be bought and planted in mid- or late autumn, snowdrops are more frequently sold 'in the green' in late winter and early spring, when in green leaf, as they tend to establish more easily than dry bulbs. Plant bulbs in well-drained, humus-rich, moist soil in partial shade. Set dry bulbs to a depth approximately three times their size, and 'in the green' plants to the same depth as the soil mark around them. Plants that have flowered will readily self-seed. Divide congested clumps every few years.

Superpower: **Survival**

Ginkgo

Ginkgo biloba
Native to China

The ginkgo is the last remaining relative of our planet's earliest trees – dating back to the Permian Period and the order of Ginkgoales of more than 250 million years ago. There are ginkgo fossils from the Jurassic Period and the Mesozoic Period – meaning you can view a leaf fossilized some 175 million years ago and then touch a living version from a tree growing in your garden. As a result, the ginkgo tree (also known as the maidenhair tree for the resemblance of its leaves to maidenhair fern) is considered a living fossil – an ancient plant from an era long forgotten. That would be a superpower on its own but the ginkgo has another: it can survive an atomic bomb. In August 1945 in Hiroshima, Japan, ginkgo trees had been in full leaf when the blast from an atomic bomb, the epicentre of the blast just a mile away (1.6 km), scorched the earth, burning away their leaves, charring their few remaining branches and scouring their trunks of bark while completely irradiating them. Yet, within a year, ginkgo trees started to sprout shoots of green despite the radiation – growing to become a symbol of hope. Today their ability to survive man's destructive devices means they have become common sights in many city centres, thriving despite thick traffic pollution.

Appearance

If you're planning on planting a ginkgo, you need plenty of space. They will typically grow 12m (40ft) high, though some have been known to reach 30m (100ft). Smaller shrub versions (*Ginkgo biloba* 'Golden Globe', for example) are more suitable for compact gardens. While ginkgo trees are slow-growing compared to some other tree and shrub varieties, their distinctive leaves are worth the wait. These are typically fan-shaped and two-lobed, much like a webbed duck's foot, earning the tree another common name – duck foot tree. Ginkgos are deciduous, and their yellowish-green leaves turn a beautiful golden yellow in autumn, before falling.

Uses

Often grown as a garden feature, its unusual, rubbery textured, strikingly shaped leaves make ginkgo a stunning addition to any planting scheme. Tea made from gingko leaves has long been popular in Asia, with compounds also used for memory enhancement in traditional Chinese medicine. Some studies have shown the tea helps improve blood circulation and also works as an antioxidant.

Interesting Facts

• The shape of the ginkgo leaf is commonly replicated in jewellery designs.

• Queen Elizabeth planted a ginkgo tree at Kew in 2009, to recognize the 250th anniversary of the Royal Botanic Gardens.

• Every ginkgo tree has flowers from each sex, meaning it can self-pollinate.

Growing Tips

This low-maintenance tree grows in most soil types and aspects, exposed or sheltered, if given reasonably well-drained conditions. It also tolerates atmospheric pollution, making it a good choice for urban locations. It's generally pest-free and requires no pruning, but may, rarely, be susceptible to honey fungus.

Superpower: **Cleans Radiation**

Sunflower

Helianthus annuus
Native to south-western USA and Mexico

As well as being one of the most iconic and joyous flowering plants, sunflowers can also perform an invaluable function – acting as hyperaccumulators. This means they are able to absorb high concentrations of toxic materials including zinc, copper, lead and radioactive waste from soil and water. The contaminants are stored in the leaves and stems of the sunflower, which can later be cropped and disposed of safely. Fields of sunflowers were planted in the wake of the Chernobyl and Fukushima nuclear disasters, in Ukraine and Japan respectively, to help reduce toxin levels. Once fully grown, sunflowers were harvested and destroyed through a process called pyrolysis, which effectively burns off the plant's organic carbons, leaving the waste metals to be stored safely without re-releasing them into the atmosphere. This process can be repeated over a period of decades until the soil improves. The technique of using living plants to clean air, soil and water, while still in its infancy, is known as phytoremediation. The term is an amalgam of the Greek *phyto* (plant) and Latin *remedium* (restoring balance). Its effectiveness depends on the concentrating effect from hyperaccumulators to bioaccumulate chemicals in their foliage.

Appearance
Vibrant flowerheads, up to 2m (7ft) high, guarantee sunflowers are a garden, patio or balcony focal point. The flowerheads grow 7–12cm (3–5in) in diameter, and have bright yellow 'petals' (actually individual flowers) known as 'ray flowers'. Depending on variety, the colour of these flowers varies from their typical golden yellow to orange, rust, brown, white and even cream.

Uses
When not saving the planet, the sunflower's day job is just as essential – the production of sunflower oil, which is a good source of polyunsaturated fat for the human diet; it helps reduce cholesterol and lowers the risk of heart disease. The giant, sun-like blooms help hungry pollinators, and its seeds are a great source of food for birds.

Interesting Facts
• Sunflower heads track the path of the sun over the course of the day, a process known as heliotropism, where they bend progressively westward.

Growing Tips
Annual varieties bloom throughout summer into autumn, taking 11–18 weeks to produce flowers when grown from seed. Sow seeds fortnightly from mid-spring in a sunny, sheltered spot in fertile, weed-free, moist but well-drained soil, for a regular supply of flowers throughout the summer. If sown in modules, plant out after hardening off and give protection from slugs and snails. Water well and regularly until established. Taller varieties may need staking. If growing for height, feed every two weeks with a nitrogen-rich fertilizer, switching to a high-potassium one just before plants start to flower.

Superpower: **Colour-Changing**

Hydrangea

Hydrangea macrophylla and *H. serrata*
H. macrophylla is native to Japan and Kazan-retto
H. serrata is native to Japan and Korea

Hydrangeas are especially significant in Japan, where the plants originated, because of their association with emotion and apology. This stems from a story about a Japanese emperor who presented hydrangea blooms to the family of the girl he loved, to apologize for neglecting her in favour of his business dealings. Conversely, the Victorians associated this shrub with boastfulness, bragging and vanity, because of its abundance of large round bloom clusters. But while its flowers are impressive, the true power of hydrangeas *H. macrophylla* and *H. serrata* lies in their ability to change their flower colour depending on soil type. For example, in alkaline soils (measured at above pH7), the plant is likely to bloom bright pink, while in acidic soil (below pH7) it's likely to be a deep blue. So, when you buy a hydrangea, its flower colour will depend on your local soil type when planted in the garden.

Appearance

Hydrangea macrophylla and *H. serrata* are quite similar varieties, not only because they both possess that special colour-changing ability, but also in their general appearance. Bigleaf hydrangea (*H. macrophylla*) has large clusters of blooms emerging from between large, slightly serrated leaves. It bears flowers in white, pink, blue or lilac, depending on the pH of the soil. Mountain hydrangea (*H. serrata*) has pink or blue flowers, which are slightly daintier than those of bigleaf hydrangea. The clusters are slightly flatter in formation, either domed or flattened, and they typically bloom from the outside inward, creating a delicate cluster of flower buds at the centre of each flowerhead.

Uses

Hydrangea really does offer year-round interest, producing beautiful new leaf growth in spring, striking summer foliage and mid- to late-flowering blooms that dry on the plant, to create a striking winter feature.

Interesting Facts

- The name 'hydrangea' comes from the plant's incredible thirst for water to power its flower production – *hydro* (water) and *angos* (vessel).
- Hydrangeas are actually poisonous. There are compounds in the foliage that, if eaten, release cyanide.
- Flowers look as if they are masses of tiny little petals, but in fact these are small leaves known as sepals, which protect the inner flower bud.

Growing Tips

In spring, buy forced flowering hydrangeas to use as houseplants in cooler spots, then transfer them outside in a permanent place in early summer. Hydrangea grows well in dappled shade in moist, well-drained soil in a sheltered position. Keep well-watered, especially during periods of drought. Leave spent flowerheads on the plant overwinter, and so avoid spring frost damage on young growth. Then prune lightly in mid-spring to just above the top set of buds formed under the dead flowerhead, as cutting below those top buds would remove the current season's flowers. Mulch in spring with leafmould or other organic matter.

You can alter the flower colour of your hydrangeas *H. macrophylla* and *H. serrata* by adjusting the pH in your soil: by adding lime powder to your soil you can lower its acidity, thus changing the blooms from blue to pink; and by adding aluminium sulphate to raise the soil's acidity you can create bluer blooms. It's best to use a soil-testing kit before you start.

Superpower: **Shapeshifting**

Holly
Ilex aquifolium
Native to the UK, Europe and North Africa

There is something magical about holly's ability to change its appearance, specifically the shape of its leaves. Common holly (*Ilex aquifolium*) happily grows lush, emerald-green leaves with smooth edges. However, if the shrub starts getting eaten, holly will fight back. Over time, its leaves regrow with prickly edges to deter common herbivores such as deer and goats. The holly can even identify at what height its foliage is being eaten, thus saving energy by leaving the higher-up, unreachable leaves smooth, while making its lower, at-risk foliage grow back spikier. This ability to carry different kinds of foliage on one plant is known as heterophylla (variable leaves). There are many cultivated varieties of holly that have been propagated with only spiky leaves, to add foliage texture to garden planning designs: for example, hedgehog holly (*I. aquifolium* 'Ferox') has spikes around the edges and on the leaf surfaces.

Appearance
Typically, holly has spiky, plain green, glossy leaves all over. Some varieties produce variegated foliage, with a creamier green shade framing the outside of the leaves, and various shades of darker green on the inside. The shrub bears delicate, four-petalled flowers in spring; these start white but can take on hints of green, yellow or pink. They develop into the classic red berries between late autumn and mid-winter, provided the flowers have been cross-pollinated.

Uses
The holly has many uses. Primarily, it's a good hedging plant if you have deer or goats locally, as it won't get eaten. By having holly, you're effectively growing your own Christmas decorations as it makes a great plant for garlands, seasonal wreaths and sprigs, to adorn both the inside and outside of the home. It is also a marvellous plant for wildlife, providing protected nesting and winter roosting for birds, as well as being great for night-pollinating moths. Holly flowers provide nectar for bees and other pollinators, and the dry leaf litter underneath the shrub is a perfect hibernating spot for hedgehogs and other small animals.

Interesting Facts
• There is some amusing confusion with the naming of some holly cultivars: for example, *I. aquifolium* 'Silver Queen' is, in fact, a male plant, while *I.* × *altaclarensis* 'Golden King' is female.

• The holly has been historically viewed not only as a pagan symbol of fertility but also as a protection against evil.

Growing Tips
Holly is an easy-to-care-for, slow-growing shrub. Berries are produced on the female plant, so you need a nearby male plant to cross-pollinate it if you want berries. Holly grows well in moist, well-drained soil, in full sun or partial shade, and is generally pest and disease-free. It can be affected by holly leaf blight, which flourishes in cool, damp conditions and causes leaf and stem discoloration as well as leaf drop. Cut out infected stems and burn them, to avoid spreading the disease. Holly can be cut back hard and pruned to shape in early spring.

Superpower: **Brain food**

English Walnut

Juglans regia
Native from south-east Europe to south-west China

The fruit of the walnut resembles the human brain, both in its general shape and in its swirling features. Because of this, walnuts have historically been claimed as a brain food. Studies have found that α-linoleic acid and linoleic acid, as well as polyphenolics and more, improve memory, cognition and motor function. There is also evidence that polyunsaturated fatty acids found in walnuts can reduce oxidative stress, neurogenesis, and more, making them fantastic at improving brain health. Additionally, compounds in the nuts include tryptophan and amino acid aid in the body's production of serotonin and melatonin – both of which play a crucial part in sleep regulation. Never underestimate the healing power of a good night's sleep. And, as modern dietary science has revealed, their potent mix of omega 3 fatty acids, vitamins and minerals can indeed have many benefits for the human body – including tackling oxidants, good gut health, anti-ageing and, importantly, combating heart disease. Anything that can improve cardiovascular health has a marked significance in reducing the risk of neurodegenerative diseases and age-related decline in cognition. It's no wonder evidence suggests humans may have started eating walnuts over 45,000 years ago.

Appearance

Walnut trees can take up to 200 years to grow to maturity and may reach 15.25m (50ft) in height, developing massive trunks more than 2.5m (8ft) thick. Their lush, green leaves provide food for caterpillars of several moths, and the nuts are eaten by mammals, including mice and squirrels, the latter's storing habits acutely helpful for the tree's propagation. The nuts themselves develop in a pitted shell surrounded by a fibrous, leathery casing which splits when they ripen in autumn. They can be eaten at this stage but tend to have a rubbery texture so it's better to dry them which will also mean they keep well.

Uses

The nuts can be eaten alone or used as ingredients in other foodstuffs like cheeses, breakfast cereals or as toppings or stuffings.

Interesting Facts

- Shakespeare wrote in *Hamlet*: 'I could live in a walnut shell and feel like the king of the universe.'
- Never put walnuts in your compost bin; there is a compound in them that is toxic to some plants such as tomatoes, potatoes, peppers and petunias. This is known as allelopathy and is stronger in black walnuts than the English walnuts.
- China and the US are the world's two largest walnut producers.

- The Latin name *Juglans* is believed to derive from *Jovis glans*, meaning 'Jupiter's acorn' or 'Jupiter's nut'. The Romans associated certain trees with their gods, and, in this case, the mighty walnut tree was linked to Jupiter, the king of the gods.

Growing Tips

Walnuts require a large space, preferring good, fertile soil that is moist but also well-drained and not in a frost pocket. Alkaline soil is preferred, as is an open site in full sun. They are best planted away from other plants, as they produce a compound known as juglone, which can affect neighbouring plants.

Superpower: **Clones Itself**

Mother of thousands

Kalanchoe daigremontiana
Native to Madagascar

As its common name suggests, this unique succulent has the ability to propagate vegetatively – effectively cloning itself by making an exact genetic copy of the parent plant – via hundreds of tiny plantlets that develop along its leaf margins. Like miniature lifeboats or escape pods from a space sci-fi movie, these are ready to drop off and recreate the plant exactly, even if it's not in trouble. When mature, they fall to the ground, each a little plant in its own right, leaves ready to photosynthesize and produce energy, and small roots creating more life as they take hold in the soil.

Appearance
Its plump green stems and fleshy, curling, sawtoothed, arrowhead leaves, blotched with purple on the undersides, make this frost-tender, perennial succulent easy to recognize. Along the leaf margins are tony rosette plantlets. In the right conditions, the plant may produce greyish-pink, dangling flowers in winter; these last formonths.

Uses
In frost-prone areas, mother-of-thousands can be grown as an indoor plant in a conservatory or greenhouse, providing hundreds of baby plants that can be propagated and given away.

Interesting Facts
• The genus name, *Kalanchoe*, is supposedly derived from a phonetic transcription of the Chinese phrase *kalan chauhu* (that which falls and grows).
• Mother of thousands was one of the first plants to be taken into space. The plant was brought aboard the Salyut Soviet space station in 1979, to boost morale, by caring for and propagating the plantlets.
• All parts of this species contain a toxic steroid known as daigremontianin.
• Spreads rapidly via its plantlets so it is better grown in a pot.

Growing Tips
In frost-prone areas, plant in cacti and succulent compost and place on a brightly lit windowsill, but not in full sun. When watering, sparing is best for this plant. If you're not sure if your mother of thousands needs watering, test the dryness at the edge of the soil by inserting your fingertip. Always make sure after watering that the plant pot drains excess water. Mother of thousands can spend brief periods outdoors once there is little risk of frost. Just make sure to let it adjust gradually, and similarly once you decide to bring it back in.

When baby plants fall, collect them and place onto damp kitchen paper on a saucer. The roots will become hydrated and start to grow. Then pot up the plantlets. Try to never let them stagnate in waterlogged compost, as this can cause root rot.

Superpower: **Explosive Reproduction**

Everlasting sweet pea

Lathyrus latifolius
Native to Europe and north-western Africa

A stunning flowering perennial, everlasting sweet pea has an unusual method of reproduction: it literally explodes! Well, its seedpods do, showering their contents far and wide, so giving the offspring the greatest possible chance of flourishing. Related to the traditional sweet pea (*Lathyrus odoratus*), beloved by gardeners everywhere, the everlasting variety returns every year, unlike its annual cousin. At the end of its flowering season, it creates seedpods vaguely reminiscent of pea pods but smaller and thinner (and toxic, so avoid eating). Over time, these undergo a unique process involving tension and pressure as they begin to dry out and change colour from a soft green to khaki brown. This process contracts the pods, creating so much tension and pressure inside each until, in an explosive burst, the pod reaches breaking point and showers its seeds away from the parent plant. This distance means seedlings won't have to compete for space, food and water.

Appearance
This beautiful vigorous climbing plant can reach up to 2m (7ft) in height, using its tendrils to climb a cane or trellis. With soft-green leaves, and delicate, almost unscented, purplish-pink flowers, each featuring five petals, it'll provide colour and interest between early summer and early autumn. The flowers of the sweet pea are reminiscent of flying butterflies, the soft delicate petals looking like wings. The grouping of the flowers gives the impression of clusters of butterflies gathered together.

Uses
Everlasting sweet pea and its annual cousin are very good for pollinators, especially bees and butterflies, who enjoy their sweet nectar. They are ideally grown up a pyramid of canes in a cottage herbaceous border, bringing pollinators and colour to the area.

Interesting Fact
- As well as spreading its seeds, everlasting sweet peas can also reproduce vegetatively from its taproot and rhizomes.
- The lovely sweet pea flowers have been an inspiration for one popular poet in particular: John Keats. He mentions them fondly in 'I stood tip-toe-upon a little hill'.

Growing Tips
Everlasting sweet pea grows well in most soil types but prefers well-drained soil in full sun or partial shade; it performs best when fed well, so dig organic matter into the soil to support plant health. Cut back to the ground in late autumn, and mulch the surface.

As well as having provided the very building blocks that paved the way for life on Earth – by lowering temperatures, removing carbon dioxide and producing oxygen (see Earth's original superheroes, page 20) – plants offer food and shelter for almost every species of living creature. Humans may have, on the whole, moved into houses from forests and caves, but if you look around you'll be hard-pressed not to immediately spot something wooden or otherwise plant-based in your built surroundings. Even the pages of this book, if you're reading a printed copy rather than an e-book, are created using wood pulp from trees, and ink originally came from plant dyes and tree resins. But if humans have largely moved on from their earliest origins, they remain firmly in the minority. Animals, insects and birds on the planet still largely rely on their natural environment for day-to-day survival.

A good example of how a single variety of tree can provide home and hearth, as it were, for a plethora of other creatures is the common oak (*Quercus robur*), which supports more life than most other trees. It provides a habitat for literally hundreds of insects, which in turn supply food for birds and mammals such as deer and badgers. It supports fungi, lichens and bats, which roost in old woodpecker holes or under loose bark and then feed on the insects in the tree's canopy. Without trees like the oak, dozens of other species simply wouldn't be able to sustain themselves.

Half of all plant and animal species on Earth live in rainforests, and as they contract through fires, logging, urban development and other deforestation, almost entirely driven by human economic enterprise, they are putting many species at risk of extinction. In fact, it's estimated that almost two million species are currently facing that threat – nearly double the figure of only five years ago.

Incredibly, a large portion of the world's terrestrial biodiversity is concentrated in the tree canopy alone. Scientists estimate up to half of all species live there – including birds, mammals, reptiles, insects and plants. The species diversity in the canopy is so high that scientists are still discovering new ones. As trees mature, they provide homes for insects, mammals and birds, whether in cracks and crevices in their bark, in nesting sites in their canopy, or in cavities forged in their trunks by animals or birds. Around a third of Europe's

Plants as Habitats

forest-dwelling birds probably nest or roost in tree cavities.

But it's not just living trees and plants that provide habitat for wildlife. Some of the most important insect and micro-organism habitats are in decomposing trees and dead plants. Worldwide, forests produce and decompose around 150 billion tonnes of wood every year.

Among the greenery and vegetation under the tall trees, life is equally bountiful. Smaller trees, bushes and plants all contribute to their own unique biome, providing food and shelter for a glorious panoply of species. And under them is the forest floor – a cornucopia of grasses, mosses, seedlings, mulch and fallen branches, leaves and seeds all decomposing merrily while creating micro-habitats for some of our smallest organisms.

Rainforests aside, there are countless other plant habitats around the globe, each sustaining its own unique species depending on the climate, vegetation and human interaction. Ancient woodlands, for example, contain centuries of loamy, undisturbed soils and accumulated layers of decomposing material that have created the perfect environment for communities of fungi, invertebrates,

Around a third of Europe's forest-dwelling birds probably nest or roost in tree cavities.

insects, mammals and birds. Unfortunately, they have been badly denuded over the centuries.

Many hedges are ancient or species-rich, and still used as boundary lines around fields or gardens. They offer a semi-natural habitat, sheltering and providing food for invertebrates, birds and mammals. Whereas once hedges were on the decline, due to the industrialization of agriculture through mechanization and the growth of mega-farms, today landowners are once again putting hedges back as a way of encouraging pollinators and other wildlife.

The planting of orchards in which humans could grow fruit dates back to the Romans and earlier. Enormously varied habitats such as these are excellent for many types of birds and insects, as are urban trees and woodland, parks, domestic gardens and any safe green pathways through cities.

Superpower: **Calm and Relaxation**

Lavender

Lavandula
Native from Macaronesia to North Africa to the
Mediterranean, Arabian Peninsula, Iran and India

The power of lavender as an uplifter of moods in humans goes way back in history. With its anti-stress and antiseptic properties, the Romans used it to scent their public baths and to help dress wounds. They also cooked with it, utilized it as an insect repellent and washed with it. Closer to home, the Elizabethans, who rarely washed, disguised their bodily stench with it. Today cosmetic shops all over the world carry lavender oils, massage rubs and other soaps and scents, making it a market worth hundreds of millions of pounds a year.

Lavender is considered nature's organic mood booster, and is similar in effect to the drug diazepam in combating anxiety, promoting calmness and reducing stress and tension. Lavender fragrance has been shown to reduce anxiety and trigger relaxation in the limbic system of the brain, which controls emotional responses and behaviour. It can also aid rest and help those suffering from insomnia.

And different varieties help in different ways. *Lavandula angustifolia* is reputed to better benefit relaxation thanks to its subtle fragrance and higher camphor levels. Alternatively, *L. intermedia* has a stronger fragrance which stimulates and energises, whilst boasting better anti-bacterial and anti-fungal properties.

Appearance
Lavender produces flowers ranging from light to dark purple, white and pink. They are tightly bunched together at the ends of long bare stems, and these flower spikes create a striking effect. Flowers fade in autumn, leaving the silver/green leaves and stems with a frosted appearance, adding subtle colour to a bed, border or tub.

Uses
Lavender soaps and oils can be purchased for baths. Lavender can also be infused into drinks, from summer cocktails to gins and tonics. It can even be used to flavour ice cream and chocolate, and be baked into cakes. The flowers can be dried and tied in bunches to scent pillows, beds, wardrobes and clothes drawers.

Interesting Facts
• Lavender was used in the seventeenth century to mask the scent of death from the Great Plague.
• It's thought the English word lavender may derive from the Latin word *lavare* (to wash).
• Loved by pollinators such as bees and butterflies – a blooming lavender bush can support hundreds of bees.
• Between mid- and late summer, massive fields of lavender as far as the eye can see are a stunning floral sight across warm Mediterranean regions.

Growing Tips
Plant in free-draining soil in full sun. Tender lavenders, such as French lavender (*L. stoechas*), should be given winter protection and grown in a sheltered spot. Cut back immediately after flowering, to retain shape and prevent becoming leggy; always avoid pruning old wood as the plant will not be able to regenerate.

Superpower: **Speed of Seed to Food**

Cress

Lepidium sativum
Native from Europe to central Asia and
Himalaya, Egypt and the Arabian Peninsula

The superpower of cress is its sheer speed of growth, from seed to vegetable ready for consumption in a very short time. Packed with nutrients, vitamins and dietary minerals, it can germinate within 24 hours and become an edible plant in 10–14 days. What you are eating with cress is the seedling stage of the plant, each sprout with its with its two infant leaves.

Even in this young state, the plant has more folate than a banana, more vitamin C than an orange, and more vitamin K than broccoli in like-for-like quantities. It also contains active biological compounds such as polyphenols and glucosinolates, which support the body against heart disease and cancers. In addition, being galactagogue (promoting breast milk in postpartum women), anti-diabetic, anti-carcinogenic, anti-asthmatic and anti-diarrhoeal, this is a healthy vegetable.

Appearance

Cress has a very simple appearance, like most plants at such an early gestational stage. Thin white stems hold up two juvenile leaves (dicotyledon), with each small plant growing in close quarters to create a miniature valley of green.

Uses

Cress makes a perfect garnish with a peppery flavour – ideal for salads, burgers, sandwiches, soups and sushi. When picked fresh and placed between buttered granary toast slices filled with creamy scrambled egg and a sprinkling of salt and pepper, cress contributes to a perfect, tasty combination.

Interesting Facts

• It's one of the best plants to teach children about growing food, as it grows so quickly.
• Cress comes in different flavours, some of which have a strong, spicy taste.
• Cress is related to watercress (*Nasturtium officinale*), which is also packed with nutrients, vitamins and minerals) and the mustard plant (*Sinapis alba*).
• Cress seeds do not even need soil to germinate; they can grow on anything that can keep them moist, from damp kitchen paper to cotton wool.
• It can be great fun to grow cress in a cleaned-out and dried eggshell, providing a wonderful green hairdo once you've drawn a face on it!

Growing Tips

This is a quick and easy crop to grow indoors, ready to harvest within just two weeks of sowing. Sow in a seed tray or pot in soil or on absorbent damp material, then cover with a clear polythene bag or clingfilm and place on a bright windowsill. Keep the compost or substrate moist. If growing outside, treat the plants as a 'cut-and-come again' crop until they start to flower, at which point they should be pulled up and composted. Outdoor plants can be grown only between spring and autumn, whereas indoor plants can be grown year-round.

Superpower: **Camouflage**

Living stones

Lithops
Native to southern Africa

Visually unlike any other plant, the plump ovoid body of living stones does not look like any typical leaf, stem or branch. Instead, at least at first glance, it appears to be a pebble. This succulent's superpower is this clever camouflage, which keeps it safe from hungry herbivores grazing the ground in its native habitat. Because the camouflage is so effective, new species of *Lithops* are still being discovered. It's believed they share common ancestors with cacti. However, while cacti evolved thorny barbs and sharp spines to deter predators, living stones matched itself to its habitat by disguising itself.

Appearance

Each lithops plant comprises two thick, fleshy, fused leaves – redolent of an upside-down hoof – designed to hold the water that the plant needs to survive. The leaves have a fissure across the top, from which new leaves and flowers emerge. Fragrant, daisy-like flowers sometimes appear in summer in yellow or white, in mature specimens. After they die back, new leaves will emerge from the central fissure, replacing the old. The leaves are fenestrated, meaning they are partly translucent to allow light to reach their interior surfaces for photosynthesis to occur. These so-called leaf (epidermal) windows are patterned in various shades of cream, grey and brown, with darker areas, dots and lines, according to species and local conditions, to camouflage the plant against its background.

Uses

This remarkable plant can be grown at home on a brightly lit windowsill.

Interesting Facts

• Some people think some varieties of living stones look like small brains because of their patination. They've also been compared to cheeky little bottoms, owing to their midline cleft.

• Living stones can live for 40 –50 years. Plus, they're very low-maintenance, as they can stay happily in the same container for up to 20 years before needing to be divided or repotted.

• The botanical name *Lithops* comes from Ancient Greek: *lithos* (stone) and *ops* (face).

Growing Tips

Plant living stones in cacti and succulent compost. They're usually grown with three to five per pot. They can also be grown from seed. Living stones love a sunny spot on a south- or east-facing windowsill – the light helping them to maintain their stone-like markings. Five hours of sunlight a day is a good target. Water them sparingly with a mister or in the sink and let the compost drain fully. Never let them sit in water as this can lead to rotting. Between mid-autumn and late spring, reduce watering to nearly nothing. Living stones are very tactile; in fact, you can tell if they need watering by appearance: if plump and hard, they're well-watered; if they're soft and wrinkled, they're thirsty.

Superpower: **Oxygen Producer**

Perennial ryegrass

Lolium perenne
Native to Macaronesia, northern Africa, Europe to Siberia
and the Himalayas

When regularly mowed and occasionally fed and weeded, the lawn is a lustrous garden carpet that supports a huge range of human activities and wildlife. The average lawn can contain between 5 and 7 different varieties of grass, meaning they are their own diverse ecosystems. Yet its superpower is not as a mere plaything, but rather as the lungs of the garden thanks to the abundance of plants that make it up.

A hectare (2.47 acres) of healthy lawn turf produces more oxygen than 1 hectare (2.47 acres) of rainforest, generating enough oxygen to sustain around 150 people a day. The process of photosynthesis is turbo-driven in lawns because they are made up of many thousands of individual plants. There can be between 50,000-100,000 blades of grass, and 100 individual grass plants per square metre of lawn. These are not only producing oxygen, but also capturing carbon and sequestering it in their roots at a rate that puts most trees to shame.

They also absorb noise; help purify water as it drains through the grasses; help keep your garden cool in hot weather; and provide a biome for millions of tiny plants and insect species to thrive.

Appearance

One of the most popular varieties for a lawn is perennial ryegrass, chosen for its high natural resistance to wear and tear. This grass has long, blade-like leaves that grow in dense tufts, with a glossy appearance, making your lawn look vibrant and healthy.

Uses

The lawn plays a significant part in the garden for reducing flooding, as it filters excess rain into the ground; it is also a valued habitat source for many creatures. It is so important to the biodiversity of the garden, from worms to microorganisms and insects to birds. The lawn provides food, shelter and moisture.

Interesting Facts

- Palm trees are more closely related to grass than most other trees.
- The first cultivated lawns were often found around castles. These areas were kept clear of trees, and grass was grown instead, for foraging animals and to keep the line of sight clear in case of attack.

Growing Tips

Regular maintenance is the key to keeping a traditional lawn in year-round peak condition. Start regular mowing with the mower blades on the highest setting when the grass begins to grow again in early spring; avoid mowing during periods of drought. Do not cut the grass too short as this encourages shallow roots, which are more susceptible to drought damage. On each mowing aim to remove no more than one-third of the lawn's height.

Rake the lawn vigorously in early or mid-autumn with a spring-tined rake, to remove old grass clippings and other accumulated debris from the grass.

Spiking the lawn with a garden fork or a hollow-tined aerator also helps it cope with drought as it helps air and water reach the grass roots and should only need doing every two or three years. Apply a top dressing of mixed loam, sand and well-rotted organic matter to fill the aeration holes.

Superpower: **Prehistoric Flowers**

Magnolia

Magnolia
Native to south-eastern USA, and west as far as Texas

Magnolias are some of Earth's earliest flowering plants. Their ancestors were blooming during the Cretaceous Period 142–65 million years ago, before the appearance of the bees and other flying pollinators that we now take for granted, so they evolved a clever way to spread and receive pollen. Firstly, they have precocious flowers, meaning they appear on the plant in spring before the leaves emerge. This makes them more prominent, uncluttered by foliage and easier to access. Secondly, the flowers produce a large quantity of pollen for hungry beetles. The flowers open in the first light of day and the stigmas become receptive to the pollen dusted on them from other magnolias on the body of visiting beetles. As the sun goes down, the outer part of the flower, the tepal, closes around the inner part, the carpel. This traps the beetles inside for the night. It is then that the female part of the flower closes and the male part of the flower becomes active, covering the beetle in pollen as it fights to get out. The next morning the flower opens, and the beetle escapes to pollinate other magnolia trees. This cross-pollination minimizes self-pollination and in-breeding, expanding healthier new plants and new varieties.

Appearance

Wonderful as either a shrub or a showstopping ornamental tree, a magnolia is sure to impress visitors to the garden. The goblet-shaped blooms stand tall atop the stems, typically in shades of white, pink and even yellow. Some varieties still produce their striking flowers ahead of their foliage, creating a vivid display to enjoy, whilst others are now deciduous. The early flowers are curled up into a vertical cigar shape, the white-flowering varieties appear at this stage as if the plant is holding hundreds of candles. Taking from ten to twenty years to reach maturity, depending on variety, you can enjoy these lush garden plants for a long time.

Uses

• Some varieties' flowers appear before the foliage making it a cheerful spectacle to uplift the heart in the new season.
• An extract of magnolia bark has been used for a thousand years in traditional Chinese and Japanese medicine for treating maladies ranging from asthma to headaches and muscle pain.
• The petals of the variety *Magnolia soulangeana* can be used in cooking, consumed fresh, roasted, pickled, dried, and even used in tea. They are said to have a deliciously powerful clove and ginger flavour.

Interesting Facts

• Magnolia was named in honour of the French botanist Pierre Magnol by the Swedish botanist Carl Linnaeus in 1737.
• One of the first records of magnolias grown as ornamental trees refers to the Aztecs during the reign of Emperor Montezuma (1502/3–20).

Growing Tips

The magnolia is relatively maintenance-free once it is established. Plant in full sun or partial shade ideally in a sheltered spot. There are large and small varieties so check the height before committing to your planting location. The plant's preference is for acidic or semi-acidic free-draining soil.

Superpower: **Sustenance**

Apple tree

Malus domestica
Native to central Asia, Afghanistan and Xinjiang Uygur
Autonomous Region of China

Proverbially, eating an apple a day might keep the doctor away, but how about ensuring the dietician is happy, too, because apples can help you lose weight. How's that for a superpower? Consuming these tasty fruits (there are more than 7,500 varieties worldwide) can slow digestion. Essentially, apples make you feel fuller, thus sending messages to your brain to stop eating.

Delicious pples are a cheap and convenient source of fibre and beneficial antioxidants, plus polyphenol plant compounds such as quercetin, which has anti-inflammatory properties. This might explain studies that link regularly dining on one apple a day with a reduced risk of heart disease, asthma and Type 2 diabetes. Pectin in the apple is a type of soluble fibre that makes a modest contribution to lowering bad cholesterol, while also helping beneficial bacteria that can help prevent chronic diseases and bowel disorders. For optimum effect, you've got to make sure you eat the skin; otherwise you'll lose half the fibre and other antioxidant plant compounds, which are found in and just under the skin.

A large apple has only 115 calories and contains 5g (⅙ oz) fibre as well as Vitamin C, B6, riboflavin, thiamine, phytonutrients, antioxidants, calcium, potassium, phosphorus and pectin. Thus, an apple is a giant in healthy food delivery.

Appearance

Apple trees have quite a rugged appearance, with silvery bark that is quite rough and uneven. They create a spectacular sight in spring, once their white blossoms open and early leaves start to add refreshing colour to the garden.

Their spherical fruits can look quite different, depending on the variety you are growing. 'Bramley' apples are wide and shallow, in a bright green shade, while 'Gala' apples are smaller and more uniform, with streaked red and yellow colouring. 'Granny Smith' apples are a cheerful green.

Uses

You can juice apples, peel them or even mash them but, without a doubt, the best way to eat an apple is as nature intended: with the skin on.

Interesting Facts

• One apple a day can have 'a significant preventative effect' in lung, colorectal and digestive tract cancers, according to a review by Perugia University, Italy, published in 2016 in the journal *Public Health Nutrition*.

• Scientists at Pennsylvania University in the US found that eating two apples 15 minutes before a meal could cut calorie intake from the meal by 15 per cent (even after taking account of the calories in the apples).

Growing Tips

Unless a self-fertile variety is chosen, apple trees require another compatible apple tree (in the same or similar pollination group) to be grown nearby. The good news is that a compatible pollination group apple tree in a neighbouring garden would suffice, since bees can fly up to 5km (3 miles) to pollinate it. Prune trees in winter, cutting back to two buds above the previous years' growth. Trees can be adversely affected by codling moths; deal with these by adding greased bands to the trunk in autumn.

Superpower: **Closes Its Leaves at Night**

Prayer plant

Maranta leuconeura
Native to central and eastern Brazil

This fabulous tropical plant's ability to adapt to the rhythms of day and night has given it its common name. As night falls, the prayer plant folds its leaves upwards in a movement redolent of clasping hands at evening devotions. The action is perceptible not only because of the sight of the leaves slowly curling upwards and in on themselves, but because you may also hear a slight rustling noise. Each leaf has a joint known as the pulvinus, which expands or shrinks in response to the plant's circadian rhythm-based internal clock. This triggers a 'nyctinastic' response once darkness falls. The plant goes to sleep as its internal clock recognizes fading light levels and temperature. Equally, as the morning arrives, pressure changes and the leaves open fully again so they're approximately horizontal during the day, to maximize absorption of sunlight. This is especially helpful in their native rainforest, where there is great competition from the tree canopy. Closing upwards at night helps the plant to retain moisture in its foliage and protects the leaf surfaces from bacteria and fungal growth.

Appearance
Prayer plant reaches an ultimate height of around 30cm (12in). Its stunning, oval-shaped foliage typically boasts three colours: two shades of green – darker around the edges and lighter along the middle fold – with a bright red, fishbone-shaped outline along the veins, providing its other nickname, the herringbone plant. The undersides of the prayer plant's leaves are a beautiful red.

Its light pink flowers are small but also contain a trigger mechanism that works just once. Flowers open in the morning and wilt in the evening; they fall off if not pollinated.

Uses
The prayer plant is a popular and attractive indoor houseplant and the perfect addition to any room thanks to its decorative leaves.

Interesting Facts
• The prayer plant has rhizomatous roots, which spread out, and from which new plants emerge.
• In the rabbit's foot plant (*Maranta leuconeura* 'Kerchoveana'), the leaves are similar in shape to the prayer plant but are light green with brown spots resembling rabbit tracks.

Growing Tips
Prayer plant thrives in a consistently warm environment, needing a minimum temperature of around 15°C (59°F), in bright but indirect light and out of draughts. Water with rainwater or distilled or filtered water; never from the tap. Mist leaves daily, or stand the plant on pebbles in a tray with a dash of water in the bottom to keep humidity high. Keep compost moist at all times from spring to autumn; then water less in winter. Feed every two months with a balanced liquid fertilizer. Wipe the leaves from time to time to remove accumulated dust. If pots become root-bound, repot in spring into a slightly larger pot.

Arguments over climate change and global warming have raged for more than half a century. Even though most scientists now believe human activity is responsible for changes in the Earth's atmospheric conditions, temperature and weather patterns, the long-term effects as modelled by supercomputers are far from understood or agreed on.

Over millions of years, Earth's climate has undoubtedly changed without the help of humans. The planet has been through hot wet periods and ice ages, each leaving its traces to be studied millennia later by scientists. Yet it appears increasingly likely the current pace of transformation is greater than any experienced in the past; according to the Intergovernmental Panel on Climate Change (IPCC), the Earth is likely to warm by another 1.4–5.8°C (3–11°F) by the end of the twenty-first century. Current efforts are aimed at keeping the rise in average surface temperature to no more than 1.5°C (3°F) above pre-industrial levels, that is, before the mid-eighteenth century.

Almost certainly much of the blame lies with the burning of fossil fuels for energy – from coal-powered factories and steam trains to our current gas-guzzling sports utility vehicles (SUVs). Mega-sized gas- and coal-fired power stations have released into the atmosphere billions of tonnes of carbon dioxide, which had been sequestered underground over millions of years by trees and other plants. Thus, it's no surprise that atmospheric concentrations of carbon dioxide have steadily increased. One study measured the change from approximately 315 ppm (parts per million) in 1959 to an atmospheric average of approximately 421 ppm in 2023. And current projections are for concentrations of carbon dioxide in the atmosphere to continue to rise to as much as 500–1,000 ppm by the year 2100. Some scientists have argued that this could be a good thing – boosting photosynthesis and thus improving agricultural yields, while in turn helping sequester even more carbon as plants grow faster and bigger, thus reducing the impact of the greenhouse effect.

More causes of climate change include depleting rainforests, ancient trees and areas of woodland, meadow, grassland and savanna. A recent study estimated that, between 2010 and 2050, global deforestation alone will result in a staggering 3.5–4.2 billion tonnes of greenhouse gases entering the atmosphere – every year.

Plants and the Climate

The good news is that by planting cleverly, husbanding species and providing financial incentives, humans can all help mitigate climate change. It's been estimated that we each breathe out around 1kg (2lb) per day – or around 365kg (800lb) a year – of carbon dioxide, so we need lots more trees to offset even just our aerobic respiration – let alone any of our other major activities like travel or building or energy consumption. As the average tree can absorb around 10kg (22lb) of carbon dioxide a year, no wonder the rainforests of Brazil have been described as the world's lungs. Old trees hold much larger amounts of carbon and pollutants than their younger counterparts, so it will take decades for the sapling you replace a 200-year-old oak tree with to reach the levels of oxygen production and carbon dioxide reduction of its proud predecessor. Even simple changes like replacing fences with hedges can have a limited beneficial local impact on species and habitat.

Sadly, it's not that simple. Plant growth cannot be sustained indefinitely without other crucial elements like nitrogen and water; thus, rising temperatures – resulting in more drought and water shortages – could offset any beneficial increases.

So remember that reducing your carbon footprint really can begin at home: a lawn of 15 × 15m (50 × 50ft) produces enough oxygen every day for four people, while 0.4 hectares (1 acre) of grass makes enough for sixty-four people. Also avoid cutting trees down – and keep planting them.

Mega-sized gas- and coal-fired power stations have released into the atmosphere billions of tonnes of carbon dioxide, which had been sequestered underground over millions of years by trees and other plants.

Superpower: **Breathing Buddy**

Peppermint

Mentha × piperita
Native to Europe and central Asia

Peppermint has been used in medicine, hygiene and confectionery since ancient times, most commonly as a decongestant, breath freshener and body cleanser. Menthol, which occurs naturally in peppermint oil, is used in everything from chewing gum to toothpaste. It is obtained by freezing peppermint oil to create crystals, which are then filtered. Menthol vapours are widely used as an antidote to respiratory congestion in nasal sprays, stimulating receptors in the nostrils and the mucus membrane. The cooling sensation of the menthol makes you feel like you are breathing a higher volume of air – a helpful placebo effect given that the menthol alone does not clear congestion. The relaxing effect and feelings of relief, however, can be just as helpful in combating congestion and shortness of breath.

Appearance

Peppermint leaves with their spearhead shape and square, purple stems are distinctive enough on their own, but it is the strong aromatic scent of mint that makes them really stand out. In summer, the plant, which grows up to 1m (3ft) in height, produces fluffy-looking, purple flowers in small clusters on spikes, adding some delicate colour to accompany the revitalizing scent.

Uses

You can make peppermint tea to help with colds, coughs and sore throats, and you can inhale steam from hot water infused with mint leaves. You can buy mint oil for aromatherapy and cooling wipes, to help relieve headaches or migraine. Mints remain one of the most popular, non-chocolate, hard sweets, and mint flavouring is common in chewing gum.

Interesting Facts

• As far back as 1500 BCE, peppermint was used in remedies and recipes. Everyone from the Ancient Greeks, Romans and Egyptians enjoyed the benefits of this aromatic flowering plant.

Growing Tips

Peppermint, along with most mint varieties, spreads prolifically via its roots if not kept in check. Plant in moist, well-drained soil in full sun or partial shade, ideally in a container to prevent it becoming invasive. Cut all stems back to ground level in autumn and divide congested container-grown plants.

Superpower: **Moves When Touched**

Sensitive plant

Mimosa pudica
Native from Mexico to subtropical America

Often grown solely for its curiosity value, the leaves of the sensitive plant rapidly fold inward when touched or shaken, returning to their original position a few minutes later. This remarkable reaction, which you can see happening, is believed to be a defence mechanism against herbivores, changing the plant's appearance from a healthy look to crushed and wilted within seconds, and returns to normal later.

Sensitive plant achieves this incredible reaction by the movement of potassium and chlorine ions from inside to outside the plant cells. This triggers a movement of moisture, which keeps the cells full and firm, collapsing them at certain points and flopping the plant. The process also closes the leaves in high winds, helping the plant to reduce moisture loss from exposed foliage. Like a number of other species, sensitive plant also closes its leaves during darkness and reopens in the morning light, being controlled by nyctinastic circadian rhythms.

Appearance
Leaves grow opposite to one another from a long rib. When grown indoors, sensitive plant makes a shaggy and delicate houseplant. In its natural environment outdoors in central and southern Africa, it has a spreading, creeping habit. The sensitive plant also boasts pink flowers resembling delicate pom-poms.

Uses
Being frost-tender, sensitive plant is predominantly grown as an interesting houseplant, for positioning on a windowsill.

Interesting Facts
• The sensitive plant deploys what is termed 'rapid plant movement', encompassing a very short period, normally under a second.
• Many other plants can move, but usually far too slowly for us to see. A houseplant on a windowsill will naturally turn its leaves towards the best source of light. A willow (*Salix*) will direct its roots to find the best source of water. These movements are called 'tropism'; in the case of looking for light, it's phototropic; for water, it's hydrotropic.

• The sensitive plant is also known as the sleepy plant or touch-me-not.

Growing Tips
Although a perennial plant in the wild, as a houseplant sensitive plant can grow straggly, so it's best treated as an annual and resown fresh every year. Position it in a bright and humid location, like a bathroom or kitchen, but not in full sun.

Superpower: **Can Hunt for Shade**

Swiss cheese plant

Monstera deliciosa
Native to Mexico and Guatemala

Most plants naturally grow towards the light, an impulse known as phototropism. However, the Swiss cheese plant switches between reaching towards light and growing towards the dark in a unique survival trick. Originating in the tropical forests of Central America, it has adapted itself to become a master of its environment by developing striking holes in its leaves – hence its common name Swiss cheese plant. These prevent the foliage from being damaged by hard-falling tropical rain by stopping water from collecting on their surfaces. Also, as all plants fight for light in the canopy-covered forests, the holes let light through to its lower leaves. Finally, the holes make the plant more stable, especially in stormy conditions, offering reduced resistance to heavy gusts. But the major battle in the rainforests is for the sunlight needed by plants to photosynthesize to produce food. Here Swiss cheese plant employs its dark arts for survival: if the plant is not getting enough light, it switches from growing towards light to moving into shadow in a process known as skototropism. By seeking darkness, it grows towards light-blocking trees. On finding them, the Swiss cheese plant utilizes another ability – sending out aerial roots along its stems to begin climbing the trunk of the tree to reach the sunlight that it needs above the canopy; it then lives as a semi-epiphyte – both independently and on the tree it's attached to.

Appearance

Swiss cheese plant produces large and attractive, glossy, emerald-green leaves. The evergreen foliage emerges heart-shaped without any holes or divides, but as the plant matures the leaves tend to develop tapered sections and enclosed holes. As climbers, Swiss cheese plants can grow quite tall with supports such as moss poles or a tree. When growing in the wild it produces fruit that tastes like a cross between mango and pineapple.

Uses

The Swiss cheese plant makes a terrific, long-lasting indoor plant that pumps out fresh oxygen into the room. Not only this, but they clear toxins in the air from the room, and their refreshing green look gives a calming feeling to the environment.

Interesting Facts

• Its botanical name, *Monstera deliciosa*, translates as 'delicious monster' – the Swiss cheese plant not only grows big, but also produces edible fruit. Houseplants are unlikely to produce these.

• Most parts of Swiss cheese plant contain calcium oxalate, which is mildly toxic, so be aware of this if you have children or plant-eating pets.

Growing Tips

Place this frost-tender plant in a warm environment of at least 18°C (65°F), in indirect or dappled light, a little away from a window. Direct sunlight can scorch the leaves. Mist regularly and, in summer, water the plant weekly (every two weeks in winter), allowing the compost to dry out between waterings. Feed in the growing season with a general houseplant fertilizer. Wipe the leaves from time to time with a damp cloth, to remove accumulated dust. Repot when the plant's roots start to bulge out of the container, ideally in spring.

Superpower: **Marriage Tree**

Myrtle

Myrtus communis
Native to Europe, Macaronesia,
parts of North Africa and Pakistan

In the Mediterranean, many cultures believe myrtle to be the tree of life. Over time, it has become synonymous as a symbol of youth, purity before marriage, fertility, innocence, fidelity and true love. Thus, this flowering evergreen shrub has been associated with marriage for many hundreds of years. The Ancient Greeks considered myrtle to be sacred to Aphrodite, the goddess of love and beauty, while the Romans used garlands of it in their wedding rituals. In Christianity, myrtle was offered as a sacred sprig to the Virgin Mary, and was meant to symbolize purity and fertility, and in early Christian marriage priests would give the newly married couple a myrtle garland after the blessing. In Judaism, it's one of the four sacred plants, symbolizing good deeds, purity and protection.

The modern tradition of including myrtle in wedding bouquets was begun in 1858 by Queen Victoria's eldest daughter, Princess Victoria, who used a sprig from Osborne House, Queen Victoria's Isle of Wight home. Since then, every royal bride has carried Osborne House myrtle, symbolizing love and hope. When Kate Middleton married Prince William, her bouquet contained not only myrtle from Osborne House but also a sprig from a plant grown from the myrtle used in the late Queen Elizabeth's wedding bouquet of 1947.

Appearance
These upright, bushy, evergreen shrubs offer attractive, consistent foliage year-round, accompanied by an aromatic scent. The leaves are glossy, spear-shaped and a verdant shade of dark green. From mid- to late summer, myrtle produces masses of white flowers, some 2cm (¾in) in width, with central tufts of white stamens; these are followed by purplish-black berries.

Uses
Reaching an ultimate height of 4m (13ft) and spread of 2.5m (8ft), this shrub is a brilliant space filler. It's great to grow for fresh clippings and sprigs, to be used for floral arrangements – or even to grow for you or a family member's wedding flowers.

Interesting Facts
• Myrtle has historically been used medicinally for ailments such as haemorrhoids, peptic ulcers and inflammation. People have also treated acne with it.
• In ancient Macedonia, laurel (*Laurus nobilis*) garlands would be made to signify a battle won, while myrtle leaves were chosen if victory was gained without bloodshed.

Growing Tips
Although myrtle grows best in full sun in acid, free-draining soil that stays reliably moist, it tolerates alkaline chalky soil. It needs protection from heavy frosts and strong winds. In the right conditions, myrtle is generally pest- and disease-free. It can be grown as a hedge or be left untrimmed as a specimen plant. It doesn't require regular pruning.

Superpower: **Carnivorous**

Pitcher plant

Nepenthes
Native to Seychelles, Madagascar, south-east China to tropical Asia, and the western Pacific including north-eastern Australia

The majority of plants are able to harvest the nutrients they need from the soil or substrate and the sun. Carnivorous plants such as pitcher plant, however, have evolved to survive even when they can't take replenishment from the soil. Instead, they capture and kill prey for its nutrients. Pitcher plant deploys a so-called pitfall trap featuring a deep cavity filled with digestive enzymes and acids, which effectively functions as its stomach. If that sounds like something out of a science fiction movie, be thankful the traps are not bigger! Some pitcher plant traps are only large enough to catch flies, ants or other small insects attracted by an array of colours and scents, while others can capture larger prey including lizards, frogs and even small rodents.

Appearance
The pitcher plant resembles something you might see in a fairy story. Its pitcher, merging in colour from red at the top (to help attract insects) to green around the bottom, is attached to the plant by a stem from its base yet appears to disregard gravity and grow vertically upwards. It stands with an open lid waiting for unsuspecting insects; in the meantime, it gathers rainwater. The foliage sits above like a canopy, the large, spear-shaped leaves a bright lime-green, complementing the darker red shade of the pitcher.

Uses
The pitcher plant looks great in a bathroom, where the humidity helps it to take in moisture for its cup.

Interesting Facts
• The common name pitcher plant comes from the shape of its urn-like trap, which looks a pitcher for drinking from.
• You can feed a pitcher plant manually with dead insects.
• One species of bat on the Indonesian island of Borneo is brave enough to use the pitcher plant to sleep in. In return for a safe place to roost, droppings from Hardwicke's woolly bats (*Kerivoula hardwickii*) provide extra nutrients for their hosts.

Growing Tips
While pitcher plants can be grown outside in frost-free climates, ideally in a bog garden, in other areas this tender evergreen perennial grows best in an unheated conservatory, greenhouse or on a house windowsill with lots of direct light. Plant it in a hanging pot. It requires acidic to neutral, nutrient-poor soil and must be kept regularly watered with rainwater during the growing season, ideally by standing the pot in 2cm (¾in) of rainwater. Keep soil damp rather than wet in winter. Pitcher plant will start to die back overwinter, at which point the dead growth can be cut off. Divide and repot congested plants in spring. Plants growing outside should not need feeding as they will catch their own food in the form of flies, ants and wasps. Plants kept indoors can be hand-fed every few weeks.

Superpower: **Feline Friend**

Catmint

Nepeta racemosa subsp. *racemosa*
Native to eastern Turkey, north-western
Iran, Iraq and Transcaucasia

This attractive, easy-flowering and hardy perennial whose aromatic foliage famously attracts cats makes a fabulous border plant with an unusual twist. One whiff of the plant can induce a euphoric high among felines – and not just the domestic variety. Lions, leopards and tigers are all known to be attracted to catmint, which can trigger a whole range of unusual behaviours, from rubbing their faces on the plant, rolling on it, salivating, chewing, headshaking, licking and caressing the foliage. What gives catmint this powerful attraction is a chemical called nepetalactone, which is believed to mimic cat pheromones. Strangely, only two-thirds of domestic cats respond to the effects of this mint-like herb, so don't be disappointed if your moggy turns up its nose. However, this naturally growing, non-harmful, recreational high for the feline population remains a delightful plant to have in the garden. Catnip (*Nepeta cataria*) has a more powerful scent but is not as ornamental as *N. racemosa* subsp. *racemosa*.

Appearance
Catmint's aromatic foliage is similar in appearance to that of classic grey-green mint leaves, with a toothed edge and net-like veining. Long stems bear light purple and mauve, two-lipped flowers growing in whorls around each stem, creating a full and colourful display.

Uses
It's a delight to see cats enjoying themselves with catmint. And don't fret if you haven't got a garden; you can buy pet toys ready-stuffed with dried catmint.

Interesting Facts
• Catmint is closely related to garden mint (*Mentha*) plants, including spearmint (*M. spicata*), peppermint (*M. × piperita*; see page 90) and pennyroyal (*M. pulegium*).
• Catmint is also a great insect repellent. Some varieties are stronger than others, while catnip (*Nepeta cataria*) is also very effective.

Growing Tips
Plant in full sun on well-drained, moisture-retentive soil. Cutting back after flowering will encourage a second crop of flowers in late summer; then leave spent flowerheads overwinter for birds to eat and for ladybirds to hibernate inside. Cut back to the base of the plant in late winter, to encourage new spring growth.

Superpower: **Water Cleansing**

Waterlily

Nymphaea
Native extensively throughout the world

The waterlily is the unofficial guardian of ponds, having many unique powers that help support biodiversity – it is both a protector of wildlife and a water purifier. This aquatic herb, growing from a mass of roots, absorbs polluting nutrients including nitrates, thus starving algae blooms like blanketweed that might otherwise suffocate ponds and watercourses. Its large floating lily leaves, known as pads, which protect ponds from excessive sunlight penetrating the water, further limit algae growth while shielding fish and aquatic insects from overheating.

A beautiful plant to adorn a pond, with more than fifty species of waterlily to choose from, in various sizes and shapes, with many different flower colours, fragrances and flowering times.

Appearance

Perhaps best known from the art of Claude Monet, waterlilies are a lovely sight floating across a pond's surface. Their circular green pads, up to 20cm (8in) across, create a stepping-stone effect on the water, while their flowers in a variety of shades and shapes add a dash of colour against the green and reflections of the sky. Blooms are typically pure white with a yellow centre and pointed petals reaching upward from the centre to rest almost flat against the water on the outermost part. Waterlilies are also available with yellow, pink, red, pale orange and even purple tinting. The flowers usually last for four days but repeat-flower within the season.

Uses

The lily pads release oxygen into the water, and also act as resting places and bridges for many creatures including dragonflies and frogs. They also provide a rich biome for aquatic and sub-aquatic wildlife and insects, hiding them from predators.

Interesting Facts

- Religions such as Hinduism and Buddhism recognize the pattern of the flower closing at dark and opening in the morning to symbolize spiritual rebirth.
- Egyptians used the waterlily flower shape on pillars and altars in temples as a sign of the sun and rebirth.

Growing Tips

Waterlilies come as bare-root plants. Aim for a position in full sun. Waterlilies dislike moving water so try not to plant them too close to water features or pipe fittings. They are best planted in aquatic baskets with nutrient-poor aquatic soil; these should be lined with fine mesh, to stop the compost washing away. Place each basket on a submerged brick or bricks. Dwarf cultivars need water 30–45cm (12–18in) deep, medium cultivars require 45–75cm (18–30in) of depth, and large need between 75 and 120cm (2½–4ft) water depth. Make sure 25cm (10in) of water covers the crown; gradually remove the bricks as the plant increases in size. After a few years, waterlilies will need to be divided.

Superpower: **Seemingly Immortal**

Olive tree

Olea europaea
Native from the Mediterranean to the Himalayas, south-central China and south-eastern Africa

The olive tree is one of nature's survivors, one of the greatest of the plant world. Burn it down to the soil or chop it back and it can regrow; starve it of nutrients and water and it can survive; bake it in the Mediterranean sun for months on end, it'll thrive. There is not a lot this tree can't take.

It's difficult to date olive trees, because there's no hardwood (the older, non-living central wood of trees, darker, denser, less permeable and more durable than the surrounding sapwood) left to measure via dendrochronology (the science of tree ring dating) or by measuring isotopes. But some are estimated to be at least 2,000 years old. The oldest olive tree on the planet is believed to grow in the Cretan town of Ano Vouves, having probably been planted before Christ was born, thought to be somewhere between 2,000 and 4,000 years old, but it is hard to know for sure. But the lineage of olives goes further back than that. It's thought the olive was first domesticated as far back as the Neolithic Period between 12,000 and 4,000 years ago. And recent studies suggest the ancestors of the olive tree managed to survive even the last Ice Age, just before the Neolithic Period started. What a superhero survivor.

Appearance

Olive trees have light grey trunks, reaching up into branches of silvery-green leaves. The spear-shaped foliage is highly distinctive – being narrow and ending in a fine point. Once the frost-hardy tree is 3–5 years old, it starts producing fruit (in the right climate), which can be harvested while either green or when fully ripened and black. As olive trees get older, their trunks become more gnarled and twisted, growing to an ultimate height of 9m (30ft) in the most favourable conditions, though in containers they are unlikely to get much taller than 1.75m (6ft).

Uses

While the olive tree is famed for its survival, its fruit is better known for being doused in James Bond's martini cocktail (shaken not stirred), spread as a tapenade on a crostini, eaten as a snack with drinks or drizzled over salads in oil form.

Interesting Facts

- The name 'olive' translates to 'oil from', as the fruits produce an abundance of fine oil, which has been used in cooking, oil lamps (including for the eternal flame in the original Olympic Games) and for anointing of kings, for eons.
- Extra virgin olive oil can reduce heart disease, Type 2 diabetes, arthritis and obesity, and can treat inflammation. Plus, evidence suggests it can help in alleviating Alzheimer's Disease.

Growing Tips

Olive trees thrive in well-drained soil, in full sun in a sheltered location where they can be protected from frost over winter. They also tolerate poor conditions as long as they are regularly watered. They are ideal container trees but will reach their full potential better in the open ground. Generally, they are pest- and disease-free, but prolonged damp may weaken an olive tree, allowing in diseases such as phytophthora root rot and verticillium wilt. They may also be vulnerable to honey fungus, so avoid planting in an area where this fungus has previously affected your plants.

During really hot weather the air temperature in urban areas rises above that of the surrounding countryside – sometimes by as much as 7°C (13°F). The phenomenon – sometimes called the 'urban heat island effect' – is typically most noticeable (and uncomfortable) at night. In cities, dark, man-made surfaces such as pavements, roofs and roads absorb almost all the incoming solar radiation as heat, storing it through the day and then releasing it as night falls – when it remains trapped, especially on windless summer nights. In such areas, the heat is enhanced by the human use of cars, air conditioning, fridges and computers. As temperatures rise globally, the disparities between urban and rural areas are likely to become more pronounced, and especially adversely risk vulnerable groups such as very young children, the elderly and people working outdoors.

The good news is that our cities can be helped to keep cool by trees: these physically provide shade and block solar radiation; and maintain a cool atmosphere. A tree's canopy acts like a parasol, reflecting up to 90 per cent of the sun's rays and cooling the ground underneath. Trees also have a psychological effect on humans. Both their physical and psychological benefits explain why city parks are often packed during sunny weather, with people picnicking, resting or playing under shady trees.

And because of this, urban architects are increasingly using trees as part of their designs to counter potential heatwaves. It is an aspect of urban architecture whose direct effects are still being studied and understood. When deliberately planted to the east or west of buildings, it has already been shown that tree shade prevents solar radiation from penetrating windows and heating external walls, reducing the amount of solar energy they can store and subsequently release, also lowering the need for air conditioning and energy costs. Thus, by intercepting the radiation before it reaches buildings or the ground, trees can lower this latent heat.

Yet it is the process of evapotranspiration, referring to the evaporation of water via the stomata (pores) in leaves, that can make the biggest difference. This cools the leaves – and the surrounding environment – in a similar way to sweating in humans. Airflow over these leaves then has a cooling effect on a larger area than just the direct locality of the tree. A large oak

Plants to Cool Our Towns and Cities

(*Quercus*) tree under optimum conditions can transpire up to 151,000 litres (33,215 gallons) of water per year through its leaves. The larger the green space, the greater the impact of its cooling locally. Over an entire city, researchers have discovered that many small parks cool faster than cities with just a few large parks. Very large areas of woodland, forest or park can even trigger cloud formation and, eventually, rainfall, which cools the air further. All of which explains why tree planting is so important in urban areas and redevelopments, and why we should be including more parks and green spaces in our cities.

The bad news is that not all trees are equal when it comes to reflecting heat, and their ability to carry out mass evapotranspiration. Large, dense canopies typical of deciduous trees provide optimum protection from solar rays, while light-coloured leaves are very effective at deflecting solar radiation. (This means, in the chilly winter months, trees that lose their leaves let light through, when it is most needed to warm the ground.) A number of other factors are also at work, including the trees' ability to absorb moisture from the surrounding soil, sometimes affected by non-permeable urban surfaces

In cities, dark, man-made surfaces such as pavements, roofs and roads absorb almost all the incoming solar radiation as heat, storing it through the day and then releasing it as night falls – when it remains trapped, especially on windless summer nights.

like pavements and roads, and heavily impacted or poorly aerated soil, which makes root growth difficult. A tree suffering stress from drought will have little water to spare for transpiration, thus little cooling impact aside from its physical shade. This is why we should be replacing non-permeable pavements with ones that allow water to seep through, adding more gullies to our roads and avoiding paving over front gardens, and installing greenery on flat-roof buildings to help deflect the sun.

Superpower: **Master of Disguise**

Bee orchid

Ophrys apifera
Native to Europe, the Mediterranean and northern Iran

The bee orchid is a smart little plant which, to optimize its ability to pollinate with other bee orchids, has devised a sneaky way of attracting male bees to its flowers, hence its name. The velvety lip of its largest central petal – known as the labellum – has evolved to mimic the look of a female bee so convincingly that males fly in to try and mate with it and end up pollinating the flower. Although coated with pollen, the male bee will repeat this process dozens of times, allowing the orchids to pollinate one another (which is more than the poor bee has been able to achieve through what is known scientifically as pseudocopulation). This clever orchid has also developed a fragrance that imitates the scent of the female bee, using pheromones to help promote the plant–pollinator relationship.

Appearance

This orchid is small but delivers a striking impact. It grows up to 30cm (12in) tall, with up to ten flowers on each plant. The labellum or largest petal of the flower is in shades of yellow, red and brown. Behind the labellum are three lilac sepals, offering a lovely and colourful backdrop. Further down the plant are ovate green leaves, which grow parallel along the stem.

Uses

In their native areas, the bee orchid freely grows besides roadside verges, embankments, waste ground and open overgrown places. It is perfect for promoting and improving biodiversity in areas of scrubland too.

Interesting Facts

• The bee orchid's botanical name comes from the Greek *ophrys* (eyebrow), referencing the hairy lip of the flower, and *apifera* (carrying bees).
• Bee orchids may flower only once in their lifetime and may appear in large numbers one year but completely disappear in other years.

Growing Tips

Bee orchids prefer full sun and well-drained soil. To encourage their appearance, cut the grass and make sure all clippings are removed between mid-autumn and early spring. Stop mowing between mid-spring and early autumn, to allow the orchid to grow and flower. Resume regular mowing once the seedpods start to mature, again removing all clippings. Seeds germinate in spring and can take as long as six years to reach the flowering stage.

Superpower: **Marvel to the Mouth**

Parsley

Petroselinum crispum
Native to Europe, Morocco, Algeria, Greece
and the Mediterranean Balkans

Parsley is a small plant with a big, special ability. Gladiators in ancient Rome would eat its leaves before entering the arena to fight for their lives, believing it would give them strength, agility and cunning. Roman legionaries also chewed parsley before battle for the same reasons. In reality, it probably just removed bad breath, because the power of this plant is that chewing its leaves reduces oral odours. The chemical eugenol found in the leaves has anti-inflammatory properties, and it has been used therapeutically in traditional dentistry to treat toothaches, as an antiseptic agent and as an anaesthetic for teeth and gum treatment. Being a very green leaf, parsley has high levels of chlorophyll. Aside from helping the plant to photosynthesize, chlorophyll enjoys powerful anti-bacterial and deodorizing abilities. This is one of the reasons that parsley is often included as an active ingredient in recipes featuring powerful flavours from garlic and onion to cleanse the palate.

Appearance
Parsley's appearance varies depending on the variety – flat-leaf or curly. The flat-leaved variety has feather-like leaves, divided into several segments, each a light shade of green. The curly variety is a similar or slightly darker shade, but each leaf is bunched up into a curling mass, giving it a more decorative effect when garnishing your meals.

Uses
After a rich, spicy meal, chew the parsley leaves to nullify bad breath. Parsley also makes a refreshing drink when combined with fresh mint (*Mentha*) in boiling water. Flat parsley is more flavoursome than curled parsley, but the latter is easier to chop finely due to its shape. Curled parsley also strikes a much more attractive feature as a garnish on your meals.

Interesting Facts
• There was an old wives' tale that the only people who could grow parsley were pregnant women or witches.

Growing Tips
Parsley is happy growing in sun or partial shade, in moist, well-drained soil in a border or container. They do very well on windowsills too; just don't let the compost get permanently waterlogged. The benefit of growing them at room temperature should help to initiate speedy germination. Water regularly, especially during dry weather, and feed with liquid fertilizer in summer. Use regularly, or cut back, to prevent it becoming leggy or flowering.

Superpower: **The Tree of Memories**

Christmas tree

Picea abies (Norway spruce) and *Abies nordmanniana*
(Nordmann fir)
Native to Europe

Is there any plant more able to trigger memories than the sight and, especially, the scent of a live Christmas tree? When you smell something, you're actually breathing in millions of tiny molecules. These stimulate the millions of nerve cells high in your nostrils, known as olfactory sensory neurons, and send messages to two olfactory bulbs in the brain. These then pass on information to be further processed in the amygdala and the hippocampus, which help to create emotion, memory and learning, entwining smells with memories and emotions.

For most of us, a Christmas tree floods the brain with memories of childhood and holidays and excitement. Visual memories join with the sensory trigger of the tree's scent to create emotional memories. Thus, a Christmas tree has the superpower to unlock emotion at first sight or smell.

Appearance

The Christmas tree, also known as Norway spruce, is a fast-growing conifer that, in its natural environment, can reach 40m (130ft) tall and live for up to 1,000 years, although when grown for sale at Christmas it tends to be cut to 1.75m (6ft). With a pointed crown and triangular shape, it has the classic festive look, with dark green, strongly scented needles; however, it does drop its needles readily.

Uses

Christmas trees as a symbol of everlasting life and peace date back through many civilizations, including the Egyptians who decorated conifers and made garlands of them in honour of the Sun God Ra, a symbol of immortality as the tree remained evergreen year-round.

The Benedictine monk Saint Boniface is credited with starting the tradition of the Christmas tree. He travelled widely in what is modern-day Germany and the Netherlands, converting people from paganism, reputedly including the village of Geismar where locals gathered around a huge old oak (*Quercus*) tree dedicated to the god Thor. This annual event of worship centred on sacrificing a human, usually a small child, to the pagan god. Boniface desired to convert the village by destroying the Thunder Oak, so he chopped it down, and used a nearby fir tree as a tool of evangelization. Subsequently, fir trees were cut and hung upside down to symbolize the compassion of Christ, the inverted triangle representing the crucifixion shape and the tree points of the triangle to symbolize the holy trinity.

Interesting Facts

- The Greeks devoted the tree to Artemis, the goddess of the hunt and moon, while the Romans brought boughs into their temples during the farming and harvest festival of Saturnalia.
- Cut Christmas trees continue to drink water from the stump like cut flowers.
- Other popular Christmas trees include Nordmann fir (*Abies nordmanniana*), Fraser fir (*A. fraseri*), noble fir (*A. procera*), blue spruce (*Picea pungens*), Serbian spruce (*P. omorika*) and Scots pine (*Pinus sylvestris*).

Growing Tips

When buying a potted Christmas tree, check it has a good root system and try to avoid keeping it in an overly hot room over the festive season. Ensure it is well-watered while inside the house; also mist the leaves regularly until you are ready to move it outside. Plant in any well-drained, moist, fertile soil, in sun or partial shade. Water very well initially, and then weekly for the first year, always close to the base of the trunk.

Superpower: **Weather Predictor**

Scots pine

Pinus sylvestris
Native from Europe to the far east
of Russia, Mongolia and the Caucasus

The Scots pine's superpower is in protecting its seeds in an egg-shaped, armoured, wooden casing that remains locked until triggered by specific weather patterns. I'm referring of course to the humble pine cone, which is a lot more clever than you might think. Seed dispersal comes in many forms across the plant kingdom, from being edible and passing through animals' digestive systems (like many fruits) to the scattering of sycamore (*Acer pseudoplatanus*) seeds through their helicopter-like flight. All methods have in common that they are aimed at helping seeds move away from their parent plant in order to maximize their chances of survival and reduce competition for sunlight, soil and moisture. Pine seeds are equipped with winged coats to aid in flight, but the mother pine protects them by locking them up tight and safe in a very tough wooden structure – the cone. The tree identifies the best weather conditions – warmth and low humidity – then unlocks its cones by triggering two distinct cell types, which act as hinges to open their scales, thus allowing the seeds within to be blown free by the wind to new locations far from the parent tree. If not all the seeds are freed and the weather changes, the cone simply closes back up and can reopen when conditions improve. Pine cones take more than two years to grow on mature trees and even longer in some varieties.

Appearance
These amazing conifers can grow up to 35m (115ft) in height, making them significant features in many landscapes – some of the oldest trees are believed to be around 700 years old. Their trunks are a scaly orange-brown, and their needles are a blue-green or yellow-green (depending on variety), growing whorled around the stems.

The pine cones themselves are typically rich brown inside, and an ashier colour on the outside after exposure to the elements. Their shapes differ, but cones tend to be rounded when closed, with a scaly appearance. When open, the scales reach out from the centre, allowing the seeds to be released.

Uses
The Scots pine makes a formidable tree in a large garden or collectively in woodland and forest. Home to many creatures, it is not only a wildlife habitat but also an oxygen producer and carbon capture hero.

Interesting Facts
• Pine trees belong to a special group called gymnosperms, dating back to prehistoric times.
• They have naked seeds, meaning they are not enclosed within an ovary.

Growing Tips
Although Scots pine grows well in most soil types, it establishes faster in nutrient-rich, moisture-retentive but free-draining soil, in full sun. This tree copes well with exposed conditions and should be allowed to grow to full height. Do not trim it.

Superpower: **Resurrection**

Resurrection fern

Pleopeltis polypodioides
Native to northern South America to tropical America

The resurrection fern gets its common name from its uncanny ability to seemingly die and then come back from the dead – flaring out with new green shoots even after long periods of drought that would prove deadly to other vegetation. It doesn't actually die, but it can lose up to 75 per cent of its water, rising to as much as 97 per cent during extreme drought. Even when shrivelled to a grey-brown ball of leaves, the resurrection fern survives. For most plants, losing just 10 per cent of their water can prove fatal. When the resurrection fern reabsorbs water, its leaves uncurl and burst back into life. Scientists have estimated the resurrection fern could last as long as 100 years without water and still revive following a single exposure to rain.

It's an epiphytic fern – meaning it needs a host and grows on branches of trees, typically the oak (*Quercus*) and cypress (*Cupressus*). You will also often find resurrection fern growing on rocks. It reproduces by spores rather than seeds.

Appearance
This luscious plant boasts refreshing green fronds, which grow into short lances. The fronds have rounded ends, softening its appearance. In its drier state, resurrection fern has the appearance of a plant beyond saving: the fronds will be dry and brown, curled up into tight swirls.

Uses
This is a great fern for nestling into unusual spaces and bringing life and animation to hard surfaces like a stone wall, rock garden or outcrop. It's also a good fern for a partially shaded stumpery, embedded in holes, or branch-to-trunk spaces on old trees, injecting attractive, eye-catching green foliage. Resurrection fern has been used as a diuretic, as a remedy for heart problems and as a treatment for infections.

Interesting Facts
• Resurrection fern first evolved 570 million years ago, making it another living fossil, like the *Ginkgo biloba* tree (page 58).
• It was the very first fern in space. In 1997, a resurrection fern was taken into orbit aboard the Space Shuttle *Discovery* for astronauts to study its 'resurrection' in zero gravity.

Growing Tips
Resurrection fern can be grown on a tree or rock, and it's also a common houseplant. Plant in a terracotta pot filled with coarse sand. Ideally, place in a humid environment such as a bathroom or kitchen. Failing that, set the pot on pebbles in a saucer with a dash of water in the bottom, to help keep the atmosphere around it moist. Water just twice a year – once in spring, again in autumn.

Superpower: **Crafting Magic Wands**

Blackthorn

Prunus spinosa
Native from Europe to central Asia,
Iran and north-western Africa

Fabled in witchcraft as the preferred choice for magic wands, staffs and other enchanted artefacts, the supernatural abilities of blackthorn have long been established in folklore. In Celtic mythology, the thorns of blackthorn were held to provide protection against evil entities, while in Irish folklore the tree was said to be possessed by the ghosts of dead witches. Accordingly, you should never cut or damage the tree during the pagan festival of Samhain, which marks the end of the harvest, or during the Beltane Fire Festival; if you do, bad luck will follow. In the children's story *Sleeping Beauty*, blackthorn trees were used in the witch's spell to create a wall of thorns that the prince had to battle through to save the sleeping princess.

Appearance
Growing to a height of 6–7m (20–23ft), this deciduous shrub has long been associated with a rural landscape. Whether supernaturally empowered or not, the blackthorn is at its most magical when it blooms in early spring. Blossoms transform what can be a slightly forbidding appearance, creating a stunning, lace-like effect. Each flower has five ovate petals, with long stamens, each tipped with yellow, giving them a delicate, sensual look. But beware, the stems produce long thorns, which reach out to protect the tree's dusty blue berries in late summer through to autumn.

Uses
Blackthorn makes a practical, attractive, countryside hedge, often used as a boundary marker by farmers, and has long been planted around cemeteries. When flowering, it provides handy nesting sites for birds, as the flowers attract early insect food, and thorns protect against predators. Its bark, flowers and berries were all used in natural remedies: for example, by healers to cleanse blood via blackthorn tonics and syrups. Blackthorn is still used to craft wooden items. Its hard, pale yellow and brown heartwood is popular for handcrafted walking sticks and canes.

Interesting Facts
• The phrase 'blackthorn winter' traditionally refers to a cold patch in early spring, when hedgerows are covered in light snowfall, resembling the blackthorn blossom.
• These trees are also loved for their rich dark berries known as sloes. A distant relative of the plum (*Prunus domestica*), they can be added to gin, to create sloe gin.
• The magical blackthorn tree has been known to live for over a century.

Growing Tips
Blackthorn thrives in full sun in most types of moist, well-drained soil and copes with exposed as well as sheltered sites. Once established, it requires little maintenance other than removing suckers in late winter or early spring while the tree is dormant; however, this should be done in midsummer if silver leaf disease is prevalent in the locality.

Superpower: **Natural Insulation and Security**

Firethorn

Pyracantha
Native from southern and central Europe
to Iran, and the Himalayas to eastern Asia

Firethorn is a great protector of homes. It's a tight hugger of walls, growing under and around windows as a leaning, almost self-supporting climbing plant. As its name suggests, it boasts sharp, fair-sized thorns on its mass of branches, making it an effective deterrent against prowlers.

Not only does firethorn protect your home but it insulates it too. It can help hold heat during winter (potentially by up to 2°C/3.5°F) while keeping the house cooler in summer by absorbing the sun's rays. Inspired by the Italian training of fruits and vines on wires and walls, firethorn has been used to beautify and protect homes since the eighteenth century; it is believed to be the first ornamental wall-trained plant not grown for food consumption.

Appearance

This attractive evergreen shrub, with its beautiful white flowers, can look quite different depending on the variety. The blooms are followed by colourful berries in large umbels hanging from the branches: *Pyracantha* 'Orange Glow' bears tangerine berries, 'Soleil d'Or' has gold while Asian firethorn (*P. rogersiana*) produces fiery red ones.

The evergreen shade of the foliage also depends on the variety, with some such as 'Teton' featuring dark emerald-green leaves, while Asian firethorn is a slightly lighter olive-green shade.

Uses

You can grow firethorn as an individual shrub for a focal point of colour, train it up a wall or fence, or grow it as a hedge, for privacy. A bushier variety called 'Mohave' is best grown as a hedge. Firethorn is a perfect home for small garden birds as its thorns protect against foxes and cats. Its flowers attract insects as spring food, while the autumn berries provide sustenance later in the year, and its dense foliage give year-round shelter.

Interesting Facts
• This plant is used to make walking sticks in India and has been cultivated into bonsai in Japan.

• Firethorn berries are so favoured by birds that they are spread to many unweeded sites such as along railway lines and in yards, disused car parks and grasslands, where the berries, having passed through the birds' digestive systems, take root.

Growing Tips

Firethorn grows in partial shade if given free-draining, moisture-retentive soil; however, it produces more berries if planted in full sun. It needs tying to a wall or support, and can be trained espalier style against the side of a house.

If plants are the planet's single most important asset in ensuring the sustenance and survival of humanity, soil comes a very close second. And the two are inextricably linked, both in the creation of the latter and in its protection. It's fair to say that, for most species, without plants there could be no soil. Even with the rise in hydroponic technology and vertical farms where everything from tomatoes (see page 144) to strawberries can be grown under artificial light in a nutrient-rich liquid, more than 90 per cent of all our food derives in some part from the soil.

Soil is the world's greatest habitat, succouring the vast majority of terrestrial flora and fauna. In fact, 59 per cent of all Earth's species live in soil: 90 per cent of the world's fungi, 85 per cent of plants and more than 50 per cent of bacteria. It is made up of, you guessed it, dead and decaying plant matter in greater and lesser quantities depending on the type. Soil is also a significant carbon sink – accounting for something like 69 per cent of the carbon stored in the world's forests. And as well as all that, it is the medium that the majority of trees and other plants grow in – the life-giving, nutrient-providing substrate that literally supports their foundations.

Forests and woodlands also create soil through the long-term decomposition of their organic matter and the action of their roots in breaking up the parent rock below the surface. Additionally, the microorganisms that live around their roots feed on the organic matter and help break it down, inserting nutrients into the mixture and binding it together into a rich compost. This humus mixes over hundreds of years with organic matter to create a rich layer of substrate that encourages further growth in a wholly virtuous circle.

Sadly, topsoil is actually an endangered resource globally, as a result of intensive farming practices, deforestation and rising temperatures. Some scientists even warn that we are losing our topsoil faster than it can regenerate. This has the potential to impact agriculture, food production and ultimately our food security. It can take up to 1,000 years to produce just 3cm (1¼in) of topsoil, so we must carefully husband it and prevent soil erosion by wind, rain, flooding and livestock.

Trees prevent so-called 'splash' erosion by intercepting heavy rainfall. They absorb a large amount of moisture – 1,500–2,000 litres (330–440 gallons) a year – help regulate the water table and

Plants Against Erosion

The shade from trees and larger shrubs helps stop the soil drying out, thus reducing the risk of wind erosion and providing habitats for smaller species of plants that live in their shade, all of which help bind the soil together.

stop flash flooding and the run-off that turns rivers brown after heavy rain as topsoil is washed away. Trees break up the wind, thereby reducing wind erosion. On top of all this, their roots physically bind the soil together and prevent it breaking up through any of these natural climate occurrences. The shade from trees and larger shrubs helps stop the soil drying out, thus reducing the risk of wind erosion and providing habitats for smaller species of plants that live in their shade, all of which help bind the soil together.

Typically, soil erosion is a slow, natural process. However, following artificial deforestation, through logging, burning or clearing to create pasture, scientists have observed soil erosion speeding up as a number of variables come into play: reduced canopy cover to protect against rain, wind and sun; splashing, flooding and drying of soil; and a loss of ground cover dependent on the trees for protection and of the root systems that bind the soil. It's not just in agricultural areas, either. Coastal sites are at risk of erosion, as sand dunes, clifftops and beaches can be highly vulnerable to wind and wave erosion. Fortunately, this can be mitigated using salt-tolerant plants and grasses with clumping root systems to physically hold the substrate in place and, in the case of sand dune habitats, prevent them blowing away. Such vegetated areas absorb and dissipate wave energy, rather than reflecting or redirecting waves onto beaches or neighbouring properties.

Recent years have also seen tree-planting campaigns in areas at risk from erosion or flooding. As new woodlands mature, they will increasingly prevent soil erosion or flooding and help keep the substrate healthy.

Superpower: **Longevity, Durability and Strength**

Common oak

Quercus robur
Native to Iran, Turkey to the Caucasus and Europe

In mythology, the oak has been venerated for millennia as the tree of gods and kings, worshipped by the pagans and employed as a symbol of strength, invincibility and endurance by mortal rulers. This giant of the tree world, producing one of the most durable timbers on the planet, was worshipped by the druids – the word druid may even have Celtic roots, meaning 'knower of the oak tree' – who practised their rites in oak groves. It's been associated with the Norse god Thor, the Roman god Jupiter, the Greek god Zeus, the Slavic god Perun and the Celtic god Dagda. Ancient kings and Roman emperors wore crowns of oak leaves and the oak is a symbol of strength and also associated with fertility. In the mid-seventeenth century, couples would be married under an oak tree – the acorn being a symbol of regeneration. Power, justice, endurance and honesty are all also symbolized by this mighty tree. Many of these associations and beliefs are connected by lightning – being one of the tallest trees across the landscape, oaks are often hit by lightning, which has added to their sacred association. Their phenomenal growth, regeneration and incredibly long lives have all embellished their mythology. They have inspired generations with their their superpower: strength and endurance.

Appearance

Growing up to 40m (130ft) in height, oaks have been a feature of the countryside for centuries. They tend to have large crowns, distinctively towering over thick, wide trunks, with bright green leaves, each with 4–5 deep lobes and smooth edges. Each leaf has only a short stem, which is what gives the tree such a full and luscious appearance. Flowers hang down from the tree as catkins. Eventually, an oak produces seeds in the form of acorns, 2–2.5cm (¾–1in) long, starting lime-green and then darkening to their distinctive brown shade.

Uses

From construction to furniture production, the strength and beauty of hardwood oak is prized globally. As an ornamental tree, it's a generational planting choice, because these trees can live for more than 1,000 years; they take forty years or more just to mature and start producing acorns.

Interesting Facts

- One of the oldest oaks is located in the heart of Sherwood Forest, Nottinghamshire, UK. The Major Oak, as it is known, is thought to be 800–1,100 years old. According to local folklore, it marked the camp of Robin Hood and his Merry Men.
- In the late 1700s, it took around 4,000 oak trees, some 40 hectares (100 acres) of forest, to construct a single ship. Entire forests were denuded to create a fighting fleet.
- Oaks trees can support hundreds of different species of insects and birds.

Growing Tips

Oaks thrive in well-drained soil high in organic matter in full sun. Keep newly planted trees well-watered during the first two years, to help them establish a strong root system. Mulch around the base of each tree, to suppress weed growth and retain moisture. Prune while oak trees are dormant, to minimize the risk of oak wilt disease; avoid hard pruning as oaks heal more slowly than other trees. They can also suffer from powdery mildew, aphids and caterpillar damage.

Superpower: **Spreads Underground**

Stag's horn sumach

Rhus typhina
Native to eastern Canada, north, central and eastern USA

The stag's horn sumach is full of surprises. In its native Canada, it grows in thickets as a result of poor soils and cold winters but, in areas with milder winters, when planted in nutritious soils, it develops as a small tree. In either situation, it maintains its abilities as a rambling survivor. Above the ground, it creates a trunk and branches, which in winter, when the leaves have fallen, are covered in soft hairs resembling antlers – hence its common name of stag's horn. But what goes on underground is even more interesting. Its roots are a mat of rhizomes (underground stems), which spread just beneath the surface of the soil. Their function is to asexually reproduce and spread. Planted in a lawn, new stag's horn sumachs will pop up as the roots spread and send up more suckers, all from the same root/ rhizome system.

Appearance

Growing up to 8m (26ft) in height, this deciduous shrub or tree produces a wonderful display to enjoy throughout the seasons. The leaves emerge from the narrow trunks in a feather-like formation, each on either side of their respective stems, hanging down. Starting verdant green, as the seasons progress they turn yellow, then bright orange, until they darken to a purplish-red before falling. The branches and stems have a slightly hairy texture. Stag's horn sumach also produces cone-shaped, yellow-green flowers in summer on the ends of the branches; these develop into dense clusters of red fruits.

Uses

When planted in a container, so the rhizomes can be contained, stag's horn sumach makes a beautiful small tree, with year-round interest and fabulous foliage. It can be used as a lawn feature. This plant is also perfect for growing as a thicket shrub. This is because it can spread readily underground from its roots, providing very dense growth.

Interesting Facts

• The flowers of stag's horn sumach have been used in clothing dyes.
• Native Americans make a lemonade-like drink from its fruits.

Growing Tips

To contain stag's horn sumach, surround its roots with a solid barrier, at least 60cm (24in) deep, to stop the roots from migrating into neighbouring lawns or flower borders. The best time to plant it is in autumn or early spring. If planted in spring, water regularly for the first few weeks. Once established, water only during periods of drought. Dig up and remove suckers as and when they become visible. If stag's horn sumach is planted in a lawn, suckers can be mown off.

It rarely needs pruning, unless space is an issue, in which case prune in early spring, but this may reduce flowers that year. Wear gloves to protect hands from the tree's skin-irritating sap.

Move container-grown specimens into a bright but cool shed or garage, for winter protection. If this is not feasible, raise the container off the ground, mulch around the tree base and wrap fleece around the container.

Superpower: **Beautiful and Edible**

Rose

Rosa
Native to the temperate and subtropical Northern Hemisphere

The range of flowers, many scented, and vibrant, glossy leaves, some with a tinge of red, make the woody perennial rose a beautiful iconic plant. A rose on St Valentine's Day signifies love. Has there ever been a plant to evoke emotions as much as the rose? It thrives in a bed, border or container – and even indoors, as far as dwarf species are concerned. Although rarely grown as a food crop, the petals of the rose are in fact edible and are packed with vitamins A, B, C, E and K, along with iron, calcium, phosphorus and antioxidants. If you'd like to eat a flavourful rose, a general rule of thumb is that, if it smells pleasant, it'll probably taste okay too. But be careful to consume only the petals, and be sure they've not been sprayed recently with garden chemicals. They can be quite delicious sprinkled on salads, as a garnish for summer meals, or chopped finely and added to butter to create spreads. Pick them in the morning, when the dew has dried from the flowers. You can also make rose-flavoured tea. It has been so popular that over time rose breeders have produced over 30,000 varieties.

Appearance
Some roses grow in a bush form, while others are climbers. Flowers range in colour from red, pink, white, orange and yellow to many more hues. Their shape varies from a blowsy cluster of petals to a flat, open flower.

Uses
Rose petals contain anti-inflammatory properties, which help calm the skin and reduce redness. They are also a cornerstone of the perfume industry, and are used in an abundance of cosmetics, in everything from oils and soaps to moisturizers and re-energizing balms. Rose water has long been used to fight bacteria on the skin and, when drunk, is said to aid digestion by easing bloating, reducing fluid retention and helping avoid constipation. To make your own rose water, dry rose petals by laying them in the sun; then store in a sealed container.

Interesting Facts
• Roses evolved in the northern hemisphere between 20 and 30 million years ago. There are fossil records of prehistoric roses.
• The ancient Egyptians recorded the rose in their hieroglyphics and bathed in rose petals.
• The Romans grew roses in their gardens, and medieval monasteries cultivated roses.

Growing Tips
Roses are best grown in ground that has never had a rose in it before. This means that the nutrients they most enjoy have not been depleted, and rose-specific diseases are not passed on from the previous bushes. Choose a sunny position and plant on top of an unpeeled banana, which will provide potassium, alongside calcium, iron, and manganese, perfect for the newly planted rose. Feed annually with a rose-specific fertilizer. How to prune and the season in which it is done depends on the type and variety of rose.

Superpower: **Self-Defence**

Willow

Salix
Native around the world, except Australia

The bark of this deciduous tree is rich in salicylic acid, which has antibiotic and antifungal properties that protect against infections. It's also been shown to prevent the growth of plants close by – a phenomenon known as allelopathy – thus reducing the risk of competition for water and light. The salicin in the tree helps repel browsing deer and many insects, too. These and other medicinal properties have been known for millennia: for example, the use of willow in pain relief is mentioned in an ancient Egyptian text dating back to *c.*1500 BCE. Traditionally, willows were sought for headaches and toothache. In medieval times, the bark was chewed to release the salicin for pain relief. Today, willow bark is sold as a herbal preparation. Its active ingredient, salicin, reduces the production of pain-inducing chemicals in your nerves. Some claim it may have a moderate effect in treating pain caused by osteoarthritis and rheumatoid arthritis. The painkiller aspirin is derived from salicin, a compound found in the bark of all *Salix* species.

Appearance

Willows can be easily identified by their classic, fairytale leaves hanging down, blowing gently in the breeze. They tend to have long, thin leaves, although some varieties (like *Salix babylonica*) have slightly rounder-shaped leaves instead. These multi-trunked trees are straight and wide, with spring shoots coming through bright green. Slender catkins are produced alongside the new leaves in spring.

Uses

Living willow branches can be readily bent to create hedges, bowers, dens, arbours and walkways. The branches are also sometimes used instead of palm branches to celebrate Palm Sunday. Certain willow species have been used historically to make cricket bats. Perfect to enjoy that gentle whack of leather on wood.

Interesting Facts

• Willows were once seen as symbols of love and happiness as well as grief, but more recently they have tended to be associated with sadness and mourning. In Shakespeare's *Hamlet*, for example, Ophelia drowns herself near a willow. It's suggested the bitter taste of willow bark has led to this connection.
• In folklore, the willow tree is believed to be quite sinister, capable of uprooting itself and stalking travellers.
• J.R.R. Tolkien's *The Lord of the Rings* featured Old Man Willow, a malign tree-spirit of great age, who tried to trap the hobbits within his roots during their journey towards Rivendell.

Growing Tips

Willows love water and should therefore be planted in reliably moist, well-drained soil, well away from a house, as roots can invade drains. Plant in full sun, and water well until established. If the plant has colourful stems, prune them almost down to the ground every spring, to encourage bright new growth.

Superpower: **Bestower of Wisdom**

Sage

Salvia officinalis
Native from south-western Germany to southern Europe

A clue to this small, compact herb's superpower comes in its name, sage, from the Old French word meaning 'wise', and the Latin *sapere*, indicating good taste and wisdom. Extracts of sage are currently being studied by scientists for their effects on human brain function, but the herb contains a variety of compounds with both biological and, potentially, neurological, benefits. Indeed, this *Salvia*'s epithet *officinalis* refers to plants with a well-established medicinal or culinary value. Traditionally, eating sage was said to improve memory and brain function, and this is probably where it gets its Latin name from. Sage is also believed to help slow cognitive decline in ageing. The hippocampus area in the brain, linked to our ability to remember, is modulated with the neurotransmitter acetylcholine. Sage is thought to aid this activity by assisting the modulation of an enzyme involved in the process.

Appearance
The attractive, aromatic, grey-green, evergreen foliage of the sage plant looks as if it is covered in a fine layer of frost, which is caused by fine hairs known as trichomes on the leaves; they are designed to protect against frost and insects. The colouring is known, perhaps unsurprisingly, as sage-green, the namesake of this classic colour. Some varieties, such as purple sage (*S. officinalis* 'Purpurea'), have a subtly purple hue to the uppermost leaves.

Sage plants also produce striking flowers, which form on towering spikes, opposite one another on the stems. These blooms are in various shades of lavender, blue-purple and rich purple, providing additional interest to these heavenly scented plants.

Uses
Sage makes a great border plant for a sunny spot, and it is perfect to harvest for adding to pasta, casseroles, stuffing, cheese and soups. Bring out the flavour by dousing the leaves with boiling water, which stimulates oils and releases more taste. Tea made from sage leaves has been brewed since medieval times as a tonic for strength, memory and wisdom.

Interesting Facts
• Sage is also a brilliant flower for pollinators.
• The Victorians grew sage in their herb gardens to signify youth, good health, friendship and a happy home.
• For generations, sage has been listed as one of the essential herbs, along with parsley (*Petroselinum*; see page 110), rosemary (*Salvia rosmarinus*; see page 134) and thyme (*Thymus*).

Growing Tips
Plant in free-draining, light soil in full sun. Prune regularly to avoid becoming leggy. Being a perennial, sage can be short-lived so take semi-ripe cuttings after a couple of years and propagate.

Superpower: **Enhanced Memory**

Rosemary

Salvia rosmarinus
Native to the Mediterranean

Ancient Greek scholars wore garlands of rosemary to enhance their memory during examinations, and Shakespeare's Ophelia in *Hamlet*, says: 'There's rosemary, that's for remembrance.' Much more recently, in 2016, people exposed to the scent of rosemary did better in cognitive tests, according to researchers from Northumbria University's Department of Psychology. Some 150 healthy people aged 65 and over were placed in rooms that had been scented with rosemary or lavender essential oils, or in a control room that had no scent. They were asked to undertake tests that assessed their prospective memory – the ability to remember to do something at a given time. Those who had been in the rosemary-scented room displayed significantly enhanced prospective memory, with test scores 15 per cent higher than those who had been in the room with no aroma.

The compound in rosemary oil believed to influence memory is cineole, thought to perform in a similar way to dementia medication , by boosting the brain's neurotransmitters. Inhalation is a fast-action way of taking medication and one of the purest (as digestion breaks down the medication ingredients using the liver), so the zesty fragrance of rosemary produces a quick boost and focuses attention.

Appearance

This woody evergreen shrub produces tall stems, each with whorled, needle-like foliage responsible for the delicious scent. Leaves are long and thin, with a refreshing green shade on the top, and a paler, almost silvery shade on the underside. It produces flowers along its stems from late spring to early summer, though some flower in autumn too. Most varieties bear delicate periwinkle-blue blooms, but some are creamy-white, such as *Salvia rosmarinus* (Albiflora Group) 'Lady in White'.

Uses

Rosemary is sometimes included in funeral wreaths as a symbol of remembrance. To activate the fragrance from a branch of rosemary, bruise the foliage between your finger and thumb, then inhale. Alternatively buy fragrant rosemary oil. Rosemary oil is also used as a hair treatment, and is said to help with thicker growth, split ends, preventing baldness and slowing the greying process.

Interesting Facts

- Napoleon Bonaparte's eau de cologne was made with rosemary.
- The botanical species name translates from Latin *ros* and *marinus* (dew of the sea), because this shrub has the ability to survive with minimal water, instead absorbing the moisture from offshore breezes.

Growing Tips

Since rosemary originates from the Mediterranean, avoid planting it in areas where temperatures drop below −5°C (23°F) and do not plant in frost pockets. It thrives in well-drained, light, sandy soil in full sun and, once established, should become drought tolerant, requiring little maintenance. Avoid over-watering it. Prune immediately after flowering, to avoid the plant becoming straggly; never cut into brown wood as the plant is unlikely to regrow.

Superpower: **Almost Unkillable**

Snake plant

Sansevieria trifasciata
Native to central Africa

The snake plant is a popular, tough houseplant that's easy to grow and tolerates drought, low-light and extreme neglect to the extent that it's often deemed unkillable. Too hot, too cold, too draughty, too dry, the snake plant can survive pretty much all these environments. Ironically, the only thing this evergreen perennial really baulks at is too much kindness – overwatering or being forced to sit in a waterlogged pot will risk rotting. This undemanding plant is also thought to ward off evil and is traditionally positioned near the main entrance to the home, to block bad spirits and energy. It also produces oxygen but, unlike most other plants, exudes this at night, because when the stomata (microscopic pores) on the plant's leaves exchange gases they do so only at night to prevent water loss via evaporation in hot climates. Thus, snake plant is a particularly good bedroom houseplant as it helps to clear toxins.

Appearance
Snake plants have earned a number of different common names thanks to the shape of their leaves, the most memorable of these being mother-in-law's tongue. The flat succulent leaves are sword-shaped and reach vertically up to a point. In the wild, they've been known to reach up to 2m (7ft) high, but those grown as houseplants typically top out at 1m (3ft). The leaves are generally variegated, which helps snake plant to regulate its temperature by absorbing a controlled amount of sunlight. Flowers vary from greenish-white to cream-coloured and have a sticky texture; snake plant is unlikely to bloom when grown as a houseplant.

Uses
Because of its reputation as a very low-maintenance, frost-tender plant, it's a popular adornment in commercial buildings and offices as well as in shopping malls, restaurants and at trade shows. As a domestic houseplant, it's perfect as an extremely long-lasting pot plant.

Interesting Facts
• Snake plant may be one of the few plants that might outlast its artificial plant rivals.
• The roots are so strong that if, over the years, you neglect to repot it the plant will remind you by bursting out of its container.

Growing Tips
When used as a houseplant, plant in peat-free, multipurpose compost, with added horticultural grit for drainage, and position in a bright spot out of direct light to avoid leaf scorch. Wait until the compost has dried out before watering, and avoid watering much, especially in winter. Never let the plant sit in water as this may cause root rot. Liquid feed monthly between mid-spring and early autumn, and wipe the leaves occasionally with a damp cloth to remove accumulated dust. If the plant outgrows its pot, repot in spring. Mealybugs may occasionally be found on the underside of leaves, in the form of white, fluffy blobs. Simply wipe off with a damp cloth.

Superpower: **Grows Without Soil**

Voodoo lily

Sauromatum venosum
Native to central Africa, the Arabian
Peninsula and southern Asia

Even by the incredible standards of the plant world, the voodoo lily is quite remarkable. Place its tuber on a warm windowsill and, regardless of soil or water, it will send up a tall, strange-looking (and smelling) spiked spadix (flower stem) over winter. This miracle flowering is possible thanks to the reserves stored in the lily's swollen brown tuber. Once it's flowered – typically creating a dramatic pattern of red, purple and yellow – you can plant it in a pot of soil in spring.

While it's certainly striking in its look, the voodoo lily's flower has another fascinating feature: its spadix emits the smell of rancid decaying meat to attract pollinating flies. Beware, a single voodoo lily can make an entire room stink. Thus, these odorous exotic plants, part of the aroid family, are doubly famous for their blooms, which are also known as corpse flowers. Other common names include monarch of the East and red calla.

Appearance
After flowering, the voodoo lily will form a single, large, deeply lobed leaf on a purple-mottled stem and roots – the latter reminiscent of spider legs – to feed its tuber for the next winter show. After being planted in warm soil, a snake-like stalk emerges. When this reaches about 60cm (2ft) in height, a single leaf unfurls, making an attractive foliage plant.

Uses
Voodoo lily makes a fascinating centrepiece for a table or room and, after flowering, an attractive addition to a patio or balcony in a container or pot. It is also a highly unusual gift plant.

Interesting Facts
• Its botanical name, *Sauromatum venosum*, comes from the Greek *sauros* (lizard), as in 'dinosaur' because of its mottled, reptilian look.
• The sap of the voodoo lily can be an irritant so wear gloves when handling.
• As it flowers, the voodoo lily heats up using a process called thermogenesis, which helps create its repulsive smell.

Growing Tips
These plants are easily grown without a container or any compost indoors. They will do well simply left to their own devices on a windowsill without soil or water in the summer. Later, you can plant the voodoo lily into a container, which will allow it to develop more foliage. These containers can be taken outside during the warmer months, (which you may want to do thanks to their pungent smell) but should be brought back indoors once the weather cools and the plant starts to die down. They will then only need moderate watering, which reduces to none in winter.

The natural compound that gives green plants their colour is at the heart of the simple yet highly effective chemical process that takes carbon dioxide from the air and, combining it with water and sunlight, creates oxygen. The compound's name is chlorophyll, and it's this modest-sounding substance that we must thank if plants are, as I argue, the planet's number one super-hero species in the fundamental and continuing survival of humanity.

We've already talked about the transformative impact of plants on Earth's atmosphere and climate (see Earth's Original Superheroes, page 20), but how about more locally? Can plants elevate oxygen levels and reduce pollutants in your own home or office? The answer, according to the National Aeronautics and Space Administration (NASA), is very much 'yes', although the conditions have to be right and it's harder to replicate laboratory results of experiments in real-world conditions. However, some houseplant species improve air quality more than others.

This enhancement is important because, on average, we spend 80–90 per cent of our time indoors, whether in workplaces or our homes. Yet the quality of the air we breathe is way down the list of priorities for scientists and policy-makers, even though we enjoy legally enforceable standards of outdoor pollution in most parts of the world. Indoor air pollution – from wood-burning stoves and fires, cigarette smoke, traffic fumes and domestic chemicals, among other invisible toxins – is believed to have killed more than three million people in 2020. It's an issue that we should be pouring research and resources into combating, especially in countries with extremely high rates of childhood asthma. Most of us, it seems, don't realize just how many pollutants might be circulating inside our homes and places of work. And the amount and type can wildly vary from house to house – every home has a different footprint.

Poor air quality is also linked to many other health conditions, including cancer, strokes, heart disease, diabetes and obesity. In addition to the personal cost of ill health, air pollution has a high cost to society, and it's often the poorest neighbourhoods that suffer the worst air quality, indoors and outside. While air purifiers with what are known as high-efficiency particulate air (HEPA) filters can help, the initial expense plus the running costs of electricity can make them too expensive for many people.

Plants for Air Quality

This is where ordinary houseplants can step in. And not just the plants themselves, the substrate (soil or compost) they grow in has been shown as an equally effective absorber of household pollutants. What's more, they can also remove particulate pollution by catching microscopic particles on leaf surfaces and stems.

NASA's highly influential *Clean Air Study*, published in 1989, looked at simple ways to remove pollutants from the atmosphere of sealed environments like space stations or underwater research laboratories. It found that certain common houseplants could provide a natural, cheap and easy way of absorbing so-called volatile organic pollutants (VOPs) such as benzene, formaldehyde and trichloroethylene. These might sound scary, but actually they're frighteningly common. Benzine is used to make plastics, resins, synthetic fibres, lubricants, dyes, detergents and pesticides, and it occurs in cigarette smoke and vehicle fumes; formaldehyde is found in paper bags, waxed papers, facial tissues, paper towels, table napkins, particle board and some synthetic fabrics; while trichloroethylene comes in printing inks, paints, lacquers, varnishes and adhesives.

Some of my particular pollutant-fighting heroes include lady palm (*Rhapis excelsa*), which takes away toxins like formaldehyde and ammonia; peace lily (*Spathiphyllum* 'Mauna Loa'), which can absorb benzene and trichloroethylene and produces oxygen; common ivy (*Hedera helix*), which is excellent at regulating humidity in indoor spaces; and the snake plant (*Sansevieria trifasciata*; see page 136), which is a superb oxygen producer and also removes xylene, trichloroethylene and benzene.

The highest oxygenating houseplants include Boston ferns (*Nephrolepis*), weeping figs (*Ficus benjamina*), aloe vera (*Aloe vera*; see page 14), spider plants (*Chlorophytum comosum*), Baberton daisies (*Gerbera jamesonii*), areca palms (*Chrysalidocarpus lutescens*), golden pothos (*Epipremnum aureum*) and money trees (*Crassula ovata*).

While some researchers insist you need a disproportionately large number of houseplants to make any measurable impact on air quality, it's always good to have them in an outdoor environment.

Superpower: **Super-Sized**

Giant redwood

Sequoiadendron giganteum
Native to California, USA

Giant redwood trees really have to be seen to be believed. Not only are they nature's largest plants – the biggest redwood in the world grows in Sequoia National Park, California, reaching an incredible 84m (275ft), and some are famously wide enough to drive a car through a hole in the trunk – but they have also adapted to be largely fire resistant. In their natural habitat, forest fires are common, cleaning the floor of dead leaves and branches without destroying these fast-growing trees. This is because redwoods have spongy bark, around 10cm (4in) thick, reaching nearly 1.25m (4ft) thick at the base of the tree, which helps protect them from flames. Also, as redwoods grow, they lose their lower branches, which stops fire from spreading into the canopy. As a result, these trees are long-living, the oldest dated between 3,200 and 3,266 years using dendrochronology (tree ring dating). Sadly, in the US they are believed to be in decline because of rising temperatures. By contrast, having been introduced into Europe in the mid-nineteenth century, they are thriving.

Appearance
As young saplings, redwoods are densely branched with conical crowns which, as they mature, become more widely spread, losing lower limbs while growing upwards. Their spongy trunks are a stunning reddish-brown, and blueish-green leaves surround brown cones.

Uses
Even though highly resistant to decay, giant redwoods are generally unsuitable as a building material because of their brittle fibres. Because of this, they haven't been logged commercially in the US for decades. Today they are best known as tourist attractions. These redwoods also provide an invaluable natural habitat for a variety of different woodland creatures and have historically been used to produce railway sleepers thanks to their rot resistance.

Interesting Facts
• The International Union for Conservation of Nature (IUCN) has listed the giant redwood as an endangered species as there are fewer than 80,000 mature specimens remaining in its native California.
• One of the reasons redwoods live so long is due to a substance called tannin in their bark, which helps deter diseases and pests, like termites.
• The tallest known giant redwood in the UK has been measured at around 54.9m (180ft) in height, still some way off Britain's largest tree, the Douglas fir (*Pseudotsuga menziesii*), which can reach up to 66.4m (217ft) in height. But the redwoods are still young so there's every chance they will eventually overtake the firs.

Growing Tips
This large, long-lived evergreen tree is utterly majestic, but not necessarily suitable for growing in a domestic garden. It thrives in areas with cool, damp summers and, although it prefers to grow in well-drained soil in full sun, it tolerates partial shade and various different soil types as well as windy and polluted sites. Water a newly planted tree regularly, until established. Giant redwood does not normally require pruning, other than to have dead and diseased branches removed once the tree is dormant, in late autumn or early winter.

Superpower: **Master of Disguise**

Tomato

Solanum lycopersicum
Native to Peru

One of our most popular home-grown food plants is the humble tomato, which has been classified as a vegetable since 1893 after a court clash over import duties into America. Until that time import tariffs had been charged on foreign fruit, but not vegetables. So a US Supreme Court case was brought by the Nix family against Edward Hedden, a port of New York tax collector, to claw back monies they'd spent importing tomatoes. While tomatoes are undoubtedly fruits – the official botanical classification defines these as entities growing from the fertilized ovary of a flower, whereas a vegetable is an edible part of a plant which is not a fruit, such as leaves of lettuce, roots of carrots, stems of asparagus or bulbs of onions – the Nix family was able to convince the Supreme Court of their cause. Deciding that usage trumped scientific classification, because tomatoes were usually served with main meals and not as a dessert, the court ruled in their favour, and tomatoes have subsequently been classed as vegetables. Cucumbers (see page 42) pumpkins, peppers, sweetcorn, peas and beans are also incorrectly labelled as vegetables when, botanically, they are all fruits. That's tax and taxonomy for you.

Appearance

Tomatoes bear bright green, lobed leaves along their stems. They produce stunningly delicate, star-shaped flowers, each with five-pointed petals, from which the fruit develops. The round or oval fruit is typically green and then darkens into fiery red, although there are many other coloured varieties, including pink, yellow, orange and even some infused with blue shades.

Uses

Tomatoes are good for human health, particularly for men and their prostate glands, as they contain a strong antioxidant called lycopene, which gives the red tomato their scarlet colouring. They can be drunk as a juice, added to salads, bruschetta and pizzas, and are an essential base in a whole host of other dishes and sauces.

Interesting Facts

• When tomatoes were first introduced into Europe in the sixteenth century, they were golden, cherry-sized and commonly known as 'little golden apples'.
• In Spain, residents throw some 150,000 tomatoes at each other in the annual festival of La Tomatina.

Growing Tips

Tomato plants can be grown either as a bush variety, trailing over the edge of a pot or hanging basket, or as a cordon – with one vertical stem tied to a cane or other support. Plant in rich soil in a sunny, sheltered spot. Water regularly as fluctuating water levels can cause the fruit to split or develop blossom end rot. Remove any sideshoots on cordons. Feed weekly with a high-potassium liquid fertilizer when plants start to flower. Once small fruits develop, remove leaves under them to allow air circulation and light to reach the tomatoes.

Outdoor tomatoes can be susceptible to blight. Look out for collapsed, shrivelled and brown leaves, stalks and stems, as well as brown marks on the fruit. Remove infected plants immediately and place in green-waste bins; never compost them.

Superpower: **Electricity**

Potato

Solanum tuberosum
Native from north-western Venezuela to western and southern South America

The humble potato is nature's battery, a store of electrochemical energy waiting to be unleashed. Researchers have claimed the low-voltage energy produced from just one good sized potato, you could charge a light-emitting diode (LED) lamp for forty days, and even charge up a mobile phone. It takes only a simple experiment, beloved of chemistry teachers globally, using a zinc nail and a piece of copper wire to power a bulb, buzzer or simple machine. Simply put, the starchy acid inside the potato undergoes a chemical reaction with the zinc and copper and, as the electrons flow from one material to another, energy is released.

Genetic studies show that the potato has a single origin, in the area of present-day southern Peru and extreme north-western Bolivia, where it was domesticated up to 10,000 years ago. As a plant, you might be surprised to learn it's from the same family as deadly nightshade (*Atropa bella-donna*; see page 22) – and, indeed, potatoes with green spots should not be eaten as they contain small amounts of toxic, as do potato shoots.

Appearance
The potato is a root vegetable developing its tasty tubers in the soil. Above ground, this herbaceous perennial has bushy green leaves, purple flowers and rises up to around 1m (3ft) high.

Uses
Potatoes are delicious when roasted, mashed or turned into fries or crisps. These tasty tubers might even have additional use for your garden to help reduce condensation. Rub a cut potato over the glass of your greenhouse, and it will stop condensation from building up. This works thanks to the starch present, acting as a barrier between the glass and the air.

Interesting Facts
• In the late 1800s, the National Carbon Company in America marketed the first dry cell battery using paste from potato starch among the ingredients.
• Potato 'eyes' are arranged in helical form, spiralling around the vegetable. Each tuber also has lenticels (small holes) that allow the exchange of gases.
• Not only is the potato the fourth most important crop grown globally, but it was also one of the first edible plants successfully grown in space.

Growing Tips
Potatoes are easy and fun to grow. Buy seed potatoes early in the year, place them in egg boxes in a cool, frost-free greenhouse or on an unheated windowsill. When the risk of frost is over, plant out into the soil, in a 15cm- (6in-) deep trench, placing them 30cm (12in) apart and leaving about 60cm (24in) between rows. Cover them with about 3cm (1¼in) of soil. As the foliage grows, move the earth up and around them, covering most of the leaves. This will encourage the plant to develop more tubers. Crop after flowering. Never plant potatoes in the same place the next year or you'll risk blight.

Superpower: **Air Purifier**

Peace lily

Spathiphyllum
Native to Mexico, northern
South America and New Guinea

According to the National Aeronautics and Space Administration (NASA), peace lilies make brilliant air purifiers as indoor plants. They can absorb airborne pollutants including benzine, carbon monoxide, formaldehyde, trichloroethylene and xylene from the atmosphere by as much as 60 per cent. They are also great at reducing levels of mould spores by absorbing and using them as food. One study by NASA found a peace lily removed more than a fifth of trichloroethylene, an irritant found in paint, carpet cleaners and varnishes, from the air in just 24 hours – more than any other houseplant. Peace lilies also absorb odours and fumes, and are one of the highest oxygen-producing indoor plants, making them an excellent choice for people suffering from allergies or asthma.

Appearance
From a stunning clump of glossy, dark green leaves, 30–60cm (12–24in) tall, a peace lily sends out white, petal-like spathes, each around a cream-coloured spadix (spike). These stand above the leaves to create a striking display that lasts for several months. The spathes turn greener as they age.

Uses
The peace lily was one of the plants included in NASA's 1989 Clean Air Study, researching ways to help keep the atmosphere in sealed environments such as space stations or undersea labs as pure as possible. Along with varieties of palm and chrysanthemums, the peace lily was found to remove all the toxins tested from the air, performing well during the study.

Interesting Facts
• Like many members of the arum family, peace lilies are poisonous, so keep them out of reach of children and pets.
• The sap can cause skin irritation so wear gloves when handling these plants.
• Peace lilies are popular among practitioners of feng shui, as they are believed to bring positive energy and an aura of calm to a home or workspace.

Growing Tips
This frost tender plant is easy to grow and relatively trouble-free when planted in peat-free houseplant compost and placed in bright, indirect light, away from any draughts. Bathrooms and kitchens, with high humidity, are ideal locations. Water regularly keeping the compost moist but not overly wet, and mist the leaves from time to time to raise humidity around the plant. Wipe the leaves regularly to remove dust build-up, which may hinder the plant's ability to photosynthesize effectively. Feed every two weeks with liquid houseplant food in spring and summer. Peace lily prefers to have its roots slightly restricted but too much root restriction will cause the plant to wilt even if watered regularly, in which case repot into a slightly larger pot filled with fresh compost.

Superpower: **Healthy Sweetener**

Sweetleaf

Stevia rebaudiana
Native from Brazil to Paraguay

Imagine there was a leaf in your garden that you could pick, pop into your mouth and enjoy a flavour just like sugar? What if this sugary-tasting leaf was calorie-free and not only safe to eat but also highly nutritious, delicious and helpful to digestion? What if it aided weight reduction, prevented dental cavities and had oral antimicrobial and antiplaque properties? What if it was safe for people living with diabetes, obesity or high blood pressure? Well say hello to the sweetleaf plant, and its extraordinary superpowers. Part of the sunflower family, the leaves contain a number of sweet-tasting chemicals known as steviol glycosides, particularly the chemicals stevioside and rebaudioside A, and can be up to 300 times sweeter than sugar cane or sugar beet. It was first used more than 1,500 years ago in Paraguay, where the Guaraní peoples know it as *ka'a he'e* (sweet herb).

Appearance

The leaves of the sweetleaf are a soft shade of green and are arranged opposite one another, creating a uniform pattern up tall stems, to 80cm (32in) in height. Each oblong leaf has a toothed edge and a midrib, which creates an upward curve.

Uses

Its aromatic leaves, which can be used fresh or dried, have been used traditionally for hundreds of years by the Guaraní peoples to sweeten tea. In the West, sweetleaf is emerging as an alternative to sugar and synthetic sweeteners but with more benefits than drawbacks.

Add freshly picked sweetleaf to your teas or summer drinks for a sugary flavour, and to salads, salsa and even main dishes and desserts. Children will inevitably take an interest in plants that grow leaves that taste like sweets, so sweetleaf is great for encouraging young gardeners.

Interesting Facts

• In Paraguay, sweetleaf is a national treasure, which is celebrated with Stevia festivals.
• It is used for many medicinal purposes, including treatments for digestion, blood pressure and for its anti-fungal and anti-carcinogenic properties.

Growing Tips

Grows well in sun or partial shade, in sandy, loam-based, well-drained soil, whether acid, neutral or alkaline. Sweetleaf is not hardy, so in frost-prone areas treat it as an annual or grow it in a pot in a cool, frost-free conservatory or on bright windowsill away from radiators. Pinch out growing tips regularly to encourage new growth. Move outside in summer and bring back indoors when temperatures start to fall in autumn.

Superpower: **Garden Bouncer**

Marigolds

Tagetes
Native to Mexico and much of South America

These cheerful, brilliantly coloured annuals and herbaceous perennials are a natural bodyguard – often sited around plants vulnerable to hungry insects. Several species' leaves secrete limonene, an aromatic airborne compound proven to have insecticidal properties that deter pests without doing any harm to them or any other insects. As a result, marigolds are often referred to as 'companion plants' and grown alongside vegetables, typically tomatoes (see page 144) and cucumbers (see page 42) and often in greenhouses, to deter whitefly. They're a favourite for a border or pot, flowering for months throughout summer and into autumn.

Appearance
Marigolds typically flower in yellows and oranges with some reds and creamy white. They vary from plain single colours to a range of contrasting markings of red, brown, yellow or orange. All marigolds have finely divided foliage, which is strongly aromatic.

Uses
All marigolds are excellent for attracting pollinating insects through their vivid hues and aromas. Studies have also shown African marigolds can have a deterrent effect on mosquitoes, sandflies, beetles, termites and even human head lice.

Marigolds have special significance in Mexico. Their golden colour and fragrance are said to help the souls of the deceased to find their way home during the annual Day of the Dead, traditionally celebrated on 1 and 2 November. Marigold petals are sprinkled along pathways and used to decorate *ofrendas* (family altars) surrounded by candles, food, personal items and photographs.

Interesting Facts
- Limonene is also found in citrus peel and in household air fresheners and mosquito repellents.
- Slugs and snails love marigolds so avoid placing them around plants that are especially vulnerable. Instead, plant them nearby as a 'trap plant' to sacrifice to slugs and snails and keep them away from your crops.

Growing Tips
Marigolds require little care when planted in reasonably fertile, free-draining soil; avoid poorly drained, heavy soil, which may encourage root rot and/or grey mould. Give plants a thorough weekly watering, and keep the soil moist during periods of drought. If grown in a pot, feed weekly with a high-potassium fertilizer from midsummer onwards. Pinch out shoots of taller cultivars, to encourage bushy growth and a neat shape. Deadhead regularly to extend flowering up to the first frosts.

Superpower: **Wish Giver**

Dandelion

Taraxacum
Native to Europe, northern Africa, Siberia and
Macaronesia

Are they weeds or wishes? That's the perennial question around dandelions with their spherical, parachute-like seedhead structures – sometimes known as blowballs – that carry the achene (seedpods). Generations of children (and adults) have made a wish while blowing away the flying seeds in one single puff (they're said to become fairies who will carry your wishes away). So while dandelions may be the bane of glossy green lawns, their bright yellow flowers are also the holder of fables and granter of wishes. They are also famed 'flower clocks', where the number of blows it takes to clear the pappus (the achene stems) of its seeds will tell the time – each puff counting as an hour. Another ancient folktale warns that, if you pick a dandelion flower, you'll wet the bed, which has quite possibly saved a lot of blooms from being decapitated. This fabled plant gets its name from its serrated foliage whose jagged edges are said to resemble the teeth of a lion, hence its French name *dents de lion*, inspiring the English name 'dandelion'. The flower's yellow ruff perhaps also resembles a lion's mane. Given their attraction to youngsters, it may be ironic that dandelion are long-lived plants, with many found in borders and amid paving stones of schools older than their pupils. They are also a familiar sight in the cracks in roads, across our lawns and borders and over hills, fields and meadows.

Appearance

The golden yellow flowers resemble miniature illustrations of the sun, their stems bursting up from a halo of toothed leaves. Dandelion flowers are more than they may at first appear – each is actually composed of several small flowers that create a full and vibrant flowerhead. Once the flowers fade, they become the recognizable pompom of fluffy white seeds, the top being a parachute that lifts the seeds in the air to spread around the surrounding area.

Uses

Both the flowers and the foliage of dandelions are edible, and contain nutrients, vitamins including A, B, C and D, plus zinc, iron, calcium and potassium. Leaves and flowers can all be added to salads, cakes and drinks. They have also been used as herbal remedies for a variety of ailments – they are said to stimulate appetite – but dandelions also make a great snack for tortoises, rabbits and other garden visitors such as caterpillars.

Interesting Facts

• North American indigenous peoples used dandelions for sore throats and tummy upsets; their foliage may also help to improve the immune system, and aid kidney function.
• Dandelion flowers are an essential early food source for waking bees before many other plants have bloomed.

Growing Tips

Dandelions tolerate all sorts of soil conditions but, when growing them for food, plant in partial shade and ensure a regular water supply to minimize bitterness. If growing in full sun, covering the leaves to exclude light for a few days before harvesting also achieves a better taste. Remove flowers before they produce seeds, to reduce the unwanted spread of these plants, which are generally pest- and disease-free.

Just as plants have provided natural remedies for millennia, subsequently inspiring laboratory-synthesized-medicines like aspirin (see willow, page 130), they have also helped provide the impetus for many modern inventions and technologies aimed at making our lives and world easier to navigate. To reflect this, the writer Janine Benyus coined the term 'biomimicry', in 1998, which means overcoming technological issues by looking for similar examples in the natural world. There are too many such discoveries to mention, but here are some of my favourites.

The hook-and-loop fastener Velcro was invented by Swiss engineer George de Mestral, after walking in the Alps in 1941 and wondering why 'sticky' burdock (*Arctium*) burrs stuck to his dog Milka's coat and his own clothing. The horticultural reason is for the purposes of seed dispersal, but having discovered how it worked, and having turned an initial annoyance into an invention, de Mestral patented his idea in 1955 ahead of its commercial introduction in the late fifties – eventually selling a reported 60 million yards (55 million metres) a year (about 55,000km/34,000 miles) in his lifetime, through a multimillion-dollar company. Originally envisioned as a clothing fastener, Velcro is today used across a wide array of industries and applications, including healthcare, construction, military and even space.

More recently, scientists at Imperial College London used computer modelling to show that by mimicking the folds of leaves on solar panels they could potentially increase energy production by around 10 per cent. It's hoped such designs will eventually inspire the next generation of green solar panel technology.

Meanwhile, also in the renewable energy sector, engineers working on wind energy have been looking at the seed structure of a maple (*Acer*) tree. Maples disperse their 'helicopter' seeds in windy conditions, sending them whirring away as the wing-shaped seed rotates aerodynamically. Today, these principles are informing scientists in making wind turbine blades more efficient and thus able to produce more electricity.

At the Massachusetts Institute of Technology (MIT) in the US, researchers have created artificial muscles that imitate the mechanism found in the tendrils of cucumber (*Cucumis sativus*) plants. These consist of coil-shaped fibres made from two polymers. The fibre coil reacts to heat by tightening up,

Plants in Contemporary Design

producing a strong pulling force. When cooled, the fibre returns to its original length. In doing so, the 'muscle' can lift many times its own weight and could eventually be used in robots, prosthetic limbs and other biomedical applications.

Another brilliant application is self-cleaning paint – inspired by the leaves of sacred lotus (*Nelumbo nucifera*), which manages to stay clean despite living largely in bogs and wetlands. Intrigued by the plant's apparent self-cleaning abilities, Wilhelm Barthlott, a biologist from the University of Bonn, led a team that discovered the leaves of sacred lotus were covered in tiny, air-trapping bumps that caused rainwater to roll off them – taking any dirt with it. Their findings were subsequently used to develop a paint that mimics this effect and, subsequently, hundreds of thousands of buildings have been coated in it to keep them looking clean.

Building design has increasingly taken inspiration from plants, too. The Esplanade building in Singapore is a terrific example, resembling as it does a giant durian, an edible fruit native to Borneo and Sumatra. Designers wanted to create a glass frontage that gave the perfect view out from every angle without turning the interior into a giant greenhouse. Their solution was to design two domed glass structures, covered with more than 7,000 pyramid-shaped, aluminium sunshades like the spikes on two halves of the durian fruit. Each side of the sunshade is a shield that opens or closes depending on the position of the sun, to ensure the interior is always kept cool.

And finally, with some 40 per cent of the world's population lacking access to sanitation, engineers have been studying whether the process by which leaves release moisture through evapotranspiration could be used to treat human waste. One solution has been the iThrone, a portable toilet whose plant-inspired membrane soaks up and evaporates the water content from human waste – reducing its mass by 90–95 per cent without the need for any plumbed-in water source, mechanical flushing or sewerage. Even for a family of five, the toilet waste needs disposing of only monthly. Four iThrones could potentially be installed for the same price as a single traditional communal toilet. Globally, this invention could one day provide safe sanitation in hard-to-reach places and slums.

So how about that – plants are so much more than just oxygenators, food products and all-round superheroes.

Superpower: **Highly Poisonous**

Yew

Taxus baccata
Native to Azores, Europe to northern Iran and north-western Africa

The yew tree has long been associated with death – and not just because it's often planted around graveyards but also because it's one of the world's most poisonous trees: two single berry stones are toxic enough to kill a child, while five will be fatal for an adult. The chemical taxine (where the botanical name for yew, *Taxus*, comes from) is a deadly cardiotoxic poison. The flesh of its bright red berries is the only part of the tree that is taxine-free. Even mushrooms growing around the base of a yew should be considered highly toxic. Symptoms of taxine poisoning include vomiting, neurological disturbance, shaking, nausea and death as a result of cardiovascular collapse. Birds however can eat the berries as their digestive system passes the seed through without causing harm, but anyone else, both human and animal, must beware. Yews were traditionally planted in graveyards, firstly because of the belief that their poison would ward off evil spirits, but secondly because their widespreading surface roots were thought to help keep the dead from rising from their graves. Finally, the roots of yew are also toxic, which helped prevent commoners grazing their cattle in graveyards. The Romans believed the yew tree could grow in hell, while both the Celts and Norse people thought it protected against spells and death.

Appearance
These small to medium-sized, evergreen trees typically grow 10–20m (33–66ft) in height, making them a striking feature. They have thin scaly bark, which comes off in flakes, and narrow, pointed, dark green leaves. The berries are known as arils, which is where a fleshy cup grows around the tree's seed tucked away inside. The yew tree's arils are bright red, standing in a colourful contrast to the dark leaves.

Uses
Yew makes a slow-growing hedge or tree of very fine quality, and can be closely trimmed to give it a formal effect in the garden. It remains the preferred choice for topiary sculptures and living arches often seen on large estates. Anti-cancer compounds from yew leaves are used in medicine today, particularly in chemotherapy treatments.

Interesting Facts
- Henry V's victory at the Battle of Agincourt in 1415 was aided by yew longbows. These were deployed by his archers, who made up around 80 per cent of his outnumbered force, and helped them outshoot the French crossbows.
- Yews are some of the oldest living trees in Europe, with some estimated at about 2,000 years old.

Growing Tips
Plant in spring or autumn in full sun or partial shade in moist but well-drained soil. Water regularly until the tree is established; avoid over-watering as this can cause root rot. Prune in summer, once established.

Superpower: **Live in the Air**

Air plant

Tillandsia
Native from southern North America to South America

Air plants really are unique: they do not rely on their roots to take in water and nutrients, nor do they need to be planted in a pot or the ground. They are incredibly low-maintenance, absorbing nutrients and water in the wild from the air and rain. They evolved in tropical rainforests, where competition for light is tough, so they developed trichomes (small scales) on their leaves, which extract water from the moisture in the air and also trap dust and debris for nutrients. Air plants are a type of epiphyte, meaning they grow on other plants without being parasitic. They perch freely on bumps or bulges in a tree trunk but take nothing from the tree other than an advantageous spot to gain light. This makes the air plant a free agent by not being anchored to the ground. The wind could blow one off its tree, or it could get knocked off by a passer-by, or a bird could even carry it away to make a nest. This makes it a great travelling plant. There are something like 650 types of air plant.

Appearance

Beautiful tufts of soft, needle-like foliage are the calling cards of certain varieties, while others have thicker or even flat and curly leaves. Leaves often have a silver surface sheen with a green appearance underneath. Also, many boast the most striking, vivid purple and pink flowers.

Uses

Air plants have become popular indoors as they are frost-tender. Being small, unobtrusive, not needing a traditional pot or soil and having the flexibility to be mounted using horticultural adhesive have encouraged a diverse and interesting trend in how to display them. Some air plants are mounted with moss on driftwood; others are enclosed in a glass terrarium or small gravel jar; while yet more are mounted on crystalline stones like amethyst.

Interesting Facts

• Air plants are always looking for high-up spots to gain access to light and nutrients. They have even been known to grow on overhead telephone wires, electrical pylons and across cliff faces.

Growing Tips

When grown as an indoor plant, position an air plant on a brightly lit windowsill. A bathroom is ideal for the moisture in the air. Otherwise, mist it with rainwater frequently in spring and summer; reduce misting in winter. Some species benefit from a dunking entirely in water for a few seconds. Shake off afterwards to shed excess water and avoid the risk of rotting. Once a month in spring and summer, add a specialist fertilizer to the water you're spraying on the leaves.

Superpower: **Defence System**

Stinging nettle

Urtica dioica
Native from Europe to eastern Asia
and north-western Africa

Without a doubt, the stinging nettle has one of the best defence systems of any plant in the world. As effective as it's fascinating, everyone who's ever got too close to a nettle, either as a child or adult, will recall the unpleasant prickly sensation of the sting, followed by the itchy rash and inflammation. Nettles can even sting through clothes. Having evolved their defence system to prevent them from being eaten or trampled, the leaves and stems alike are covered in hundreds of tiny hollow hairs, many but not all filled with formic acid and histamines – which trigger the stinging sensation in humans. The leaf tips are pure silica, an oxide of silicon and major constituent of sand, which makes them brittle, so when they make contact with the skin, they snap off, injecting their toxins. After a relatively short period of discomfort, depending on exposure to the plant, the effect wears off.

All of this makes them a plant to avoid. Yet nettles are nutritious and may offer all sorts of other health benefits, including reducing inflammation, combating hay fever and lowering blood pressure and sugar levels, so much so that they've been a staple of herbal medicine for thousands of years.

Appearance

These perennials tend to appear in large clumps and have leaves with serrated edges. The foliage is similar in shade to that of mint (*Mentha*) leaves. Nettles produce clusters of minute, drooping, white, green or purple flowers similar to catkins.

Uses

Nettles make a great habitat and food source for many butterfly species: the red admiral, small tortoiseshell, painted lady, comma and peacock all like to lay their eggs in them. Unaffected by the toxins, the caterpillars tuck into the leaves for food while the stings offer protection from predators. Night pollinator moths including the jersey tiger, mother of pearl, snout moth and burnished brass similarly utilize nettle plants.

Interesting Facts

- An old gardener's tale suggests a quickly applied dock (*Rumex*) leaf and some human saliva, rubbed into the affected area until the green colouring of the leaf is visible on the skin, will negate the effects of a nettle sting. However, it's most likely this is simply a placebo, though the evaporating moisture from the saliva and sap could offer some relief.
- Another traditional antidote is toothpaste, its antihistamines nullifying the formic acid sting, while the menthol relieves and cools the rash.
- Nettle leaves and stems make a great liquid fertilizer. Place bunches into a bucket, weigh them down with a brick and fill with water until they break down into an organic plant food.
- Gouda containing nettles and garlic is a specialty Dutch cheese, while Cornish yarg is wrapped in nettles.
- During the First World War, amid fabric shortages, the Germans and Austrian used nettles to make army uniforms.
- During the Second World War, the British used dried nettles to create dye for camouflage.
- Nettles are also commonly known as burn nettle, burn weed or burn hazel.

Growing Tips

To keep nettles in check, plant in nutrient-poor, dry soil. Wear thick gloves when harvesting leaves or cutting stems, and prune after flowering to prevent them self seeding.

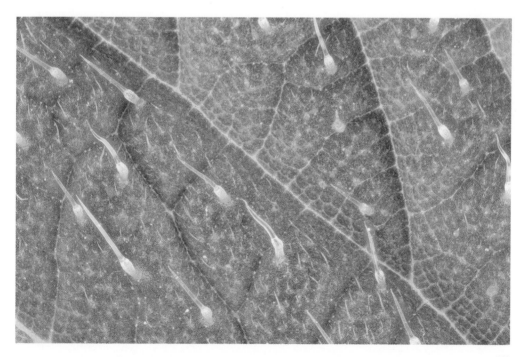

Superpower: **Underwater Predator**

Bladderwort

Utricularia
Native across the world except the Arabian Peninsula

This fascinating carnivorous plant uses tiny hollow bladders (as traps) in its underwater stems to capture and digest tiny creatures such as insect larvae, aquatic worms and water fleas. In some species, the microscopic bladders, to which its common name refers, are underwater and controlled by a flexible valve, which is typically kept closed. The remaining 80 per cent of bladderworts are grown in the earth, terrestrially. A physiological process moves moisture out of a bladder – generating a state of low pressure within. When the plant's miniature prey triggers sensitive bristles projecting from the valve door, the bladder trap suddenly opens and a quick inflow of water created by the vacuum inside sucks the unwitting creature into the bladder. This takes place in less than $\frac{1}{500}$ of a second. Within 15–30 minutes the trap is reset by passing water to the exterior while the prey is consumed inside.

Appearance
Most species form long thin stems both above and below the surface of their substrate, whether that be pond water, wet soil or moss. The bladder traps are attached to these along with some underwater leaf shoots. However, it is the flowers of the bladderwort – often the only part of the plant above water or soil, that make them such an attractive addition to a pond or garden wet area. Typically bearing two distinct lobes, they come in a variety of pale colours from whites to lavenders.

Uses
Bladderwort is incredibly good at controlling unwanted insect larvae in a fountain or small pond, while possessing attractive flowers that add an attractive aesthetic aspect. They provide an important source of nectar for pollinating species, too.

Interesting Facts
• These diminutive aquatic triffids subsidize their diet from photosynthesis with nitrogen, potassium and phosphorus from the microscopic creatures they trap and consume.
• There are approximately 233 species of bladderwort, ranging from aquatic varieties to those that thrive in wet soil.

Growing Tips
Of the three types of bladderwort, terrestrial is best grown in a water tray or in a saucer with water, year-round. They can typically be purchased either sold in a bag of water or rooted in a perforated container called an 'aquatic basket'. Epiphytic bladderwort is ideal in a terrarium or water plant baskets in water 1cm (½in) in depth. During winter keep terrestrial bladderwort frost-free and damp. Aquatic bladderwort becomes dormant over winter, dropping to the bottom of the pond until spring.

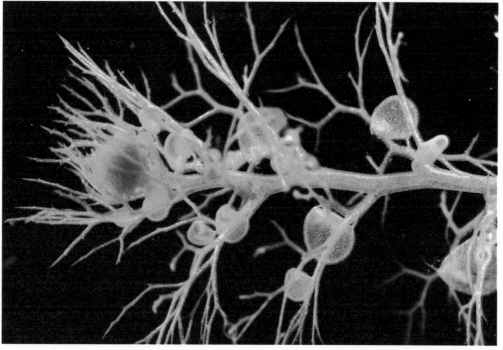

Superpower: **Gets Your Body Fitter**

Blueberry

Vaccinium corymbosum
Native to eastern Canada and central and eastern USA

Blueberries are the original superfood. Some nutritionists believe that if you make only one change to your diet it should be to add blueberries. They're high in vitamin C and a good source of fibre and they contain the compound pterostilbene, which protects the heart in the same way as cholesterol-lowering drugs. Studies show that a single 100g (4oz) portion contains the same quantity of age-defying antioxidants as five servings of other fruits and vegetables. These antioxidants can help guard the body against a range of diseases, from cancer and heart disorders to cataracts, arthritis, asthma and even age-related neurological diseases.

Compounds in blueberries known as flavonoids are believed to improve memory and general cognitive function, including reasoning skills, decision-making, verbal comprehension and numerical ability – and may even slow age-related decline associated with disorders such as Parkinson's and Alzheimer's. By preventing infectious bacteria from clinging to the wall of the gut, bladder and urethra, blueberries also offer protection against cystitis. Finally, blueberries contain polyphenols, which help guard against wrinkles and keep skin looking younger, and they help the body make collagen, which keeps skin supple. No wonder they say not all heroes wear capes!

Appearance

The spear-shaped, smooth-edged leaves are a revitalizing shade of green, and in autumn they turn striking shades of amber and red (as nutrients are mobilized back into the shoots for next year's growing). These shrubs bear wonderful, petticoat-shaped, white flowers in spring. The berries themselves cluster together on the stems, juicy blue or purple spheres with a powdery appearance on the surface. You can even grow pink blueberries, a variety called 'Pink Lemonade', which are a nice alternative for a similar flavour.

Uses

Productive blueberry bushes make attractive features in the garden. The berries are not only tasty, but a regular portion can play a part in keeping you healthier and looking younger. Eat a cupful or so a day, add to fruit salads or sprinkle over porridge or cereal. Blend with other beneficial plants such as raspberries, strawberries, currants and broccoli to make a super smoothie – a fantastic start to the day. Mixing blueberries in your morning yogurt is another health enhancer. Try freezing them into ice cubes and adding to your prosecco or soft drinks on a summer's day for a tangy bite when you get to the bottom of the glass.

Interesting Facts

• Blueberries are a truly ancient fruit. It is believed that humans have been enjoying their benefits for more than 13,000 years.
• One cupful of blueberries contains just forty-four calories.

Growing Tips

Plant blueberries in acidic moist soil in a sunny spot; in a container use peat-free, acidic (ericaceous) compost. Compact varieties such as 'Bluetta' or 'Sunshine Blue' are happy in containers. To help keep the soil acidic, water your blueberries using rainwater, rather than tap water, which is slightly alkaline. When planted in too much shade, this shrub will develop less blossom and less fruit. To ensure your crop doesn't get snatched up by birds, cover the shrub in a fine mesh. Just make sure you fasten it securely to the ground, to avoid the risk of birds getting caught underneath or trapped in its folds. Never prune your blueberry plant for the first couple of years after planting it, so that it can concentrate on producing a large crop.

Superpower: **Bringer of Thoughts**

Pansy

Viola
Native in Northern Hemisphere and much of the Southern Hemisphere

Few flowers bring a smile more than pansies. The colourings on their blooms even resemble a little face scrunched up as if in deep thought. The sight of bright and colourful flowers with complex patterns is known to stimulate neurotransmitters in our brains, such as dopamine, serotonin and hormones like oxytocin, which motivate us, promote happiness and encourage creativity and thought. The last attribute has been closely associated with this plant for centuries. The name pansy comes from the French *pensée* (meaning thought or reflection), derived from the Latin word *pensare* (to ponder). The Spanish call them *pensamientos*, again meaning thought. Even William Shakespeare added to their reputation for reflection and remembrance, having Ophelia hand them out in *Hamlet* while saying: 'And there is pansies, that's for thoughts.' Containing all the colours of the rainbow, these flowers have inspired our imaginations from childhood. Lewis Carroll's heroine Alice even meets singing pansies in the animated Disney version of her *Wonderland* adventures.

Appearance
Plants reach no more than 25cm (10in) tall, and have delicate, green, lobed leaves. Some pansy varieties have heart-shaped, overlapping petals in several colour combinations. Other pansies are available in single colours, while violas tend to be more multicoloured, featuring intricate patterns. They tend to have darker-marked centres to the blooms, which makes them all the more striking in comparison to the lighter shades of the petals.

Uses
Pansies are useful flowering bedding plants almost year-round. Varieties are bred for different seasons, with winter hybrids able to produce colourful blooms in the cold. Grow several of these plants as ground cover in a bed or container, or for variant colour in a hanging basket, to make a lovely addition to your garden. Many pansies are sweet-scented. Pansy petals are edible and are a source of vitamins A and C. They add colour to salads, and they can be crystallized with egg white and caster sugar, for cake decorations. Finally, the petals can also be drunk as a tea.

Interesting Facts
• Pansies were grown in Greece in the fourth century as components for medicines.
• If growing pansies to eat, never spray them with garden chemicals.

Growing Tips
Although perennial, pansies are best treated as an annual. They prefer damp but not waterlogged soil. Sow in early spring, or buy them grown between late autumn and late spring, ideally in a hanging basket or container, where their flowers can be appreciated. You can also sow them at the end of summer for autumn displays. Feed with slow-release fertilizer when initially planting, or use a high-potassium liquid fertilizer every two weeks, to encourage repeat flowering over a long period. Also deadhead regularly, and trim old leaves to keep plants looking good and preventing them from becoming straggly.

Superpower: **No Change Between Life and Death**

Strawflower

Xerochrysum bracteatum
Native to Australia

The appearance of strawflower blooms remains all but unchanged in death. Not only does it keep its beautiful shape and form, but it holds on to its colour too – remaining a perfect flower in its afterlife. No wonder it's also known as golden everlasting and is sometimes considered a symbol of immortality. The petals of this sturdy little plant are like stiff thin cardboard, and this is where it gains its popular common name strawflower. The outer part of the flower is not in fact made from traditional petals, but instead are modified leaves which only look like petals. These are known as bracts, which when alive protect the inner flowers and help attract insects for the purposes of pollination. They also respond to the weather, opening in dry conditions and closing when raining. When dried, the strawflower remains in the open flower position and can last for years.

Appearance

Strawflowers produce vibrant, cheerful-looking blooms – in a large variety of shades – between summer and autumn. These herbaceous perennials and annuals can grow up to 1m (3ft) in height, and their blooms can be up to 8cm (3¼in) across. The lance-shaped leaves provide a striking green backdrop to the rainbow of floral colours.

Uses

Grow these plants in your garden and enjoy their colourful flowers, which make for a wonderful display that is very attractive to pollinators. Then dry the flowers yourself so you can continue enjoying them for years to come. For drying, harvest each flower when it is looking its best; cut with sharp scissors on the lower stalk and hang upside down. This helps the flower to dry evenly with the free flow of air and keep much of its colour.

Interesting Facts

· Dried strawflowers were incredibly popular in displays in Victorian times.
· In the 1980s, small versions of the dried flowers were glued on to cacti plants and sold as perpetually flowering cacti – an unscrupulous practice that has now ceased.

Growing Tips

Plant in well-drained soil in full sun. Once established, strawflowers need very little care.

Superpower: **Fragrance Only at Night**

Night phlox

Zaluzianskya ovata
Native to southern Africa

We all know night owls, people who come to life as the rest of us are settling in for the evening. Well meet the horticultural equivalent: night phlox. This compact evergreen is pretty enough during the day but, as darkness falls, its aromatic superpower becomes apparent. The afternoon sun charges its flowers, which open at nightfall. Pure white, they reflect the moon and release the most heavenly scent. This uplifting fragrance will quite literally stop you in your tracks.

But the phlox is not doing it for our benefit. Its delights are aimed at attracting night pollinators, such as the elephant hawk moth, the white-lined sphinx moth and the carpenter bee, which bring our garden alive at night. These insects are crucial in pollination – moths being a largely underestimated contributor. There are more than 2,500 species visiting flowers at night. The scent of night phlox is intentionally strong as many night pollinators rely on their olfactory abilities to identify plants suitable for feeding. Phlox is a special treat, the perfect food source for hard-working creatures while the rest of the garden sleeps. Then, as the dawn arrives, the evening creatures retreat to their homes and the flowers of the night phlox close once again. It's magical.

Appearance

Night phlox is a naturally clump-forming, evergreen plant that typically grows no taller than 25cm (10in). Its grey-green leaves, slightly sticky to the touch, are almost holly-like, due to their serrated appearance. The flowers, which are best enjoyed in the evening, are particularly striking, with pure white petals on the inside able to reflect bright moonlight and a dark raspberry shade on the outside adding some wonderful colour.

Uses

The plant is a raised-bed favourite, lifting it higher than its fellows makes it easier for humans to enjoy the evening scent. In aromatherapy, the essence of night phlox is used to reduce stress and anxiety, and it aids relaxation and uplifts mood too.

Interesting Facts

• The night phlox's powerful scent is often compared to a combination of honey, almond and vanilla.

Growing Tips

As it's only frost hardy it may need to be moved to a sheltered spot or into a porch or greenhouse for winter. You should grow night phlox in a pot filled with well-drained, peat-free, multipurpose compost. In milder areas, it can be grown outdoors in full sun in humus-rich, moist, well-drained soil and in any aspect, exposed or sheltered. Cut back hard after flowering to maintain shape and prevent legginess.

Index

Acknowledgements

My thanks go to Fern Keyte for valuable help on research a project coordination, especially for keeping me to my deadlines. James Saker and Rosie Irving on research and Matt Nixson with research and editing. A big thanks to my publisher Philip Cooper and the team at Quarto for their professional assistance in editing, artwork and layout to create this beautiful book. Thanks to my agent Andrew Gordon from David Higham for all his kind support. Thanks to my family – Adele and our children Alice, Abigail and Lance – who constantly remind me of the value of appreciating nature in this modern world of technological distractions. And thanks to my parents Raymond and Jean, who instilled in me a love of and affection for this wonderful living world.

Quarto

First published in 2025
by Frances Lincoln, an imprint of The Quarto Group.
One Triptych Place, London SE1 9SH,
United Kingdom
(0)20 7700 9000
www.Quarto.com

Text © 2025 David Domoney
Design @ 2025 Quarto Publishing Plc

ISBN 978-1-83600-117-1
e-Book ISBN 978-1-83600-118-8

10 9 8 7 6 5 4 3 2 1

Design by Ocky Murray

Printed in China

MIX
Paper | Supporting responsible forestry
FSC
www.fsc.org   FSC® C016973

Picture credits

Shutterstock

Margaret. Wiktor 2; Pavaphon Supanantananonont 7t; Stefano Maraschio 7b; FotoHelin 9; Andreas Ardler 10; barmalini 11; NinaM 13t, Shaiith 13b; Jan phanomphrai 15t; Valentyn Volkov 15b; MarjanCermelj 16; Klopping 17; Bob Pool 18; David JC 19; Greens and Blues 23t; Oxik 23b; Nahhana 24; N.Stertz 25; SanderMeertinsPhotography 27t; Natalia Golubnycha 27b; Kumulugma 29; mangbiz 31; Uunal 32; Israfoto 33; Rudak Hanna 34; Margy Crane 35; RadekSzymczakPhoto 37; Alexander Ruiz Acevedo 40; DK_2020 41l; Ganna Zelinska 41r; adi suweca 42; itor 43; Creative by Nature 45t; Lulu's Imagination 45b; Uzo Borewicz 47t; AP Hannibal 47b; Nelly B 49t; Tai Dundua 49b; Rybnikova Olga 51t; Kuttelvaserova Stuchelova 51b; Stone36 57t; Nitr 57b; Maris Grunskis 58; Danny Ye 59; Godlikeart 61t; Oleksandr Filatov 61b; Watcharee Suphaluxana 62; Chrisseee 63; sopf 65t; Chris Andrews Fern Bay 65b; stevemart 66; Erhan Inga 67; gunawand3570 69t; Christina Siow 69bl; madhu.m 69br; Grey Zone 71; Iva Vagnerova 75t; Kotkoa 75b; iMarzi 77t; Piotr Wytrazek 77b; Boyloso 79t; Oleg Kovtun Hydrobio 79b; radresnac 80; Thirteen 81; Julia Ardaran 82; Magarnee 83; Lady_Luck 84; BongrakArt 85; Erika Kirkpatrick 87t; Stylish_Pics 87b; Dmitrii Ivanov 90; Toeizuza Thailand 91; Neelakandi 93t, 93b; adhira rar 94; UladzimirZuyeu 95; S.Zykov 97; JTKP 99t; Toeizuza Thailand 99b; Amelia Martin 101t; Georgia Evans 101b; Wirestock Creators 103t; Swisty242 103b; Kaneos Media 104; Fabio Balbi 105; Thomas Hochreutener 108; Serge Goujon 109; aniana 111; soaring4031 112; Arcaion 113; Nadya Puris 115t; losmandarinas 115b; Kathy Clark 117t; Joanne Dale 117b; HWall 119t; Iva Vagnerova 119b; Miodrag Zlatarov 121t; NataliSel 121b; muratart 124; Gulf MG 125; Alvydas Kucas 127t; Peter Klampfer 127b; MaCross-Photography 129t; fetrinka 129b; Axel Bueckert 131t; Heiko Kueverling 131b; Happy window 133t; teatian 133b; Fabrizio Guarisco 134; New Africa 135; Ije 137; COULANGES 139; NatalieJean 143; O_Lypa 145t; Toyakisphoto 145b; Skrypnykov Dmytro 147t; Homestudio 2 147b; FotoHelin 149; ESYl 150; TatianaMishina 151; MarieKaz 153t; Tatevosian Yana 153b; Philip George Jones 154; AmusingPhoto 155; Juan Carlos Munoz 159; Alf Ribeiro 160; AlejandroTT 161; anmbph 162; Lubo Ivanko 163; Lima_84 165t; D. Kucharski K. Kucharska 165b; vaivirga 166; Foodio 167; Anna Gratys 169t; Alex006007 169b; Nungning20 170; Sheila Fitzgerald 171

Getty Images

Jacky Parker Photography 5; Sashy29 70

Alamy Stock Photo

blickwinkel 53; Josephine Marsden 173